THE SEARCH FOR

RAOUL WALLENBERG –

THE TRUTH

Sharon Leontine Wallenberg

Liberty 61 Books

"The Search For Raoul Wallenberg – The Truth"

Library of Congress Cataloguing in Publication Data

Published by: Liberty 61 Books

Dedication

This book is dedicated to my Wallenberg family: Grandsons Ricky and Bobby, Daughters Rebekah and Marisa, Son-In-Law Kyle, Cousin Ann-Sophie, her Husband Mikko, and to my Parents Mary and John, Aunt Edith Wallenberg, Grandmother Emma Leontine Anderson Wallenberg, with special acknowledgement and gratitude to Creator God, Higher Power, Infinite Wisdom, Loving Kindness, for all the help, inspiration, guidance, and strength to make this endeavor and book possible…and, of course, to Raoul Gustaf Wallenberg.

Introduction

This book tells a true story which reaches back over 100 years, touches on the lives of over 100,000 people, involves the governments of four countries, includes hundreds of documents, and both exposes scandals, and showcases heroism.

There are many books about Raoul Wallenberg, but this is unique. It is about all the behind the scenes activity involved in the release of his prison records from the Soviet Union, where the idea originated, why it was important, how it was done, and the background of the impartial investigation which followed. In addition, it exposes the people who tried to prevent the truth, the reasons why, who confronted them, and those who worked tirelessly on behalf of this great hero. I know, because this is my story.

This story had its humble beginnings in Glen Cove and Sea Cliff, Long Island. The book will demonstrate what an individual can accomplish if he or she is determined, imaginative, courageous, and compassionate. Further, the book extends into the future by advocating implementation of lessons learned, avarice avoided, and compassionate lifestyles adopted.

I hope you enjoy it!

Contents

Part One – The Hero

Part Two – The Search

Part Three – Going Forward

Part One

The Hero

Chapter One: The Family

Raoul Gustav Wallenberg was a Swedish Diplomat credited with saving 100,000 innocent lives during World War II. This is his story, and his legacy.

Raoul Wallenberg was a Swedish citizen born on August 4, 1912 into the wealthy, influential, diplomatic Wallenberg family. The Wallenbergs played a prominent role in Swedish industry and political history for generations. The family controls the biggest pool of investment capital in Scandinavia. The main instrument for accumulating capital and putting it to work is the Enskilda bank. It is controlled, but not wholly owned, by the Wallenbergs.

The Wallenberg family dynasty was founded by Andre Oscar Wallenberg, a naval seaman who visited New York. He returned to Sweden determined to create a modern commercial bank. In 1865, he founded the

Enskilda bank, which became the center of the family's vast interests. Andre Oscar Wallenberg traveled throughout Europe gaining investors in Sweden's then untapped resources. These included ball bearings, compressed air machines, Swedish Match (not a dating service), L.M. Ericson (telecommunications), De Laval (dairy machines), SKF, Asea (Swedish General Electric). Stora Kopparberg, Providentia, Atlas Copco, and other diverse enterprises including steel, pulp paper, shipping, chemicals, minerals, hydroelectric power, department stores, and restaurants. They were probably the wealthiest family in Sweden.

Andre Oscar Wallenberg had five sons: Knut, Axel, Oscar, Marcus (Senior), and Gustav. Knut was the Swedish Foreign Minister during World War I. Axel was an envoy to Washington. Marcus Senior had two sons, Jacob and Marcus, who became the leaders of the Wallenberg dynasty.

Gustav was the Ambassador to Japan and Turkey, the father of Raoul Senior, and the grandfather of Raoul Gustav Wallenberg, the hero.

During World War II, Swedish neutrality consisted of Marcus Wallenberg keeping the lines of communication open with Britain, and Jacob Wallenberg doing the same with Germany. This also involved sales of Swedish ball bearings, iron ore, and other materials used in war. It should be noted, and understood, that Sweden is a very vast, and sparsely populated country, reaching all the way to the Arctic Circle. It was then (and maybe now), impossible to defend. Some people may find it offensive that Swedish neutrality is not the 'neutrality' commonly thought of in the United States. In reality, it was the only way for those people to survive. Many people seeking asylum escaped into neutral Sweden, which would otherwise not have been possible.

Before being critical, please put yourself in their shoes.

At one point, Marcus Wallenberg received threats from the U.S. that Swedish ships carrying iron ore would be bombed. Marcus had no idea if it were true or not. Jacob Wallenberg had a close friendship with Karl Goerdeler, the Mayor of Leipzig. Goerdeler was involved in a conspiracy to overthrow Hitler. The conspirators hoped for the support of Nazi Generals. Goerdeler gave the details of the plot to Jacob. The hope was that through the Wallenberg's connection with the British, the conspirators could be assured that if Hitler were overthrown, the Allies would make peace with Germany. After the failed attempt on Hitler's life, Jacob was warned never to go to Germany. Goerdeler escaped initially, but was eventually arrested and executed. Jacob's and Marcus's nephew, Raoul, had other wartime activities.

Chapter Two: Raoul

Raoul Wallenberg Senior, the Grandson of Andre Oscar Wallenberg , founder of Sweden's Wallenberg dynasty, married Maria Sofia Wising, or Maj (pronounced My). The happy couple conceived a son. Unfortunately, Raoul Senior died of cancer at age 23. He died eight months after the marriage to Maj, one week after her 21st birthday, and three months before Maj gave birth to Raoul Gustav Wallenberg.

Raoul started life with a young widow mother, and a maternal grandmother who was also a recent widow. Mother and grandmother shared a house on a beautiful island in the archipelago surrounding Stockholm. They cherished infant Raoul. Although he lost his father, Raoul remained connected to the influential Wallenberg family through his paternal grandfather, Gustav. Grandfather Gustav oversaw Raoul's education and career.

Maj, married Fredrik Von Dardle when Raoul was six years old. Von Dardle later became the Director of Karolinska, Stockholm's largest and most prestigious hospital. Maj and Frederik had two children: Raoul's half-sister, Nina Von Dardle Lagergren, and half-brother, Guy (pronounced Gee) Von Dardle. Maj and Fredrik died within two days of each other in February 1979. Nina's daughter, Nane, Raoul's niece, married Kofi Annan, the former Secretary General of the United Nations.

Raoul Wallenberg studied Architecture at the College of Architecture and Urban Planning at the University of Michigan in Ann Arbor. Although a foreign student not studying in his native language, Raoul finished the program one year early. Raoul graduated in 1935 and was awarded the outstanding Student of the Year award which was given to one student out of 1,100.

Back in Stockholm after graduation, Raoul entered an Architectural contest to design a recreation center out of an old abandoned wharf. He designed a complex with an outdoor swimming pool, and other amenities. Raoul Wallenberg won second prize. First prize was won by Sweden's leading architect of the day.

World War II brought the building industry in Europe to a halt. At his grandfather's request, Raoul took several international entry level positions. Grandfather Gustav desired to prepare Raoul for an eventual leadership role in the Wallenberg family banking business alongside his uncles Marcus and Jacob. In this capacity Raoul Wallenberg traveled to, and experienced life, in various European, African, and Middle Eastern countries, including Cape Town, South Africa, and Haifa, in then Palestine, among others.

It was during his travels, and job experiences, that Raoul saw firsthand the cattle cars filled with people in Europe. He listened to accounts of the atrocities in Europe from Jewish emigrants in Palestine.

When Raoul was 25 years old, his grandfather Gustav Senior died. Jacob and Marcus did not offer him a position in the family banking business, or any of its associated undertakings.

Upon returning to Stockholm from his international positions, Raoul Wallenberg accepted a position in an import export firm. Through the family banking and business network, Raoul was put in touch with Kalmon Lauer. Lauer had a flourishing import-export business, the Central European Trading Company. It specialized in Eastern European specialty foodstuffs. Lauer was originally from Hungary, and lived in Stockholm. He needed a reliable, knowledgeable employee who could travel freely in Europe, including Nazi occupied countries. Raoul was fluent in English, German, and Russian. With his knowledge of languages, his energy and initiative, his negotiating skills, and his attractive personality, Raoul was ideal for the job. Within eight months he became a Junior Partner and Director of the Company, and developed a close personal friendship with Lauer.

Chapter Three: American War Refugee Board

Some victims of the WWII concentration camps in Europe escaped. They were able to inform their relatives in the United States about what was happening in Europe. Their relatives in turn, contacted Henry Morgenthau, President Roosevelt's Secretary of the Treasury. Morgenthau was able to convince President Roosevelt to start an initiative to save lives. Roosevelt established the American War Refugee Board. It was funded by American tax payer dollars, and contributions from wealthy individuals.

The American War Refugee Board needed to go behind enemy lines to rescue people. This was impossible to do while the U.S. was at war with the Nazis. A Representative of a neutral nation was needed to covertly carry out the operations of the American

War Refugee Board. To that end, the United States contacted Sweden, Switzerland, Turkey, and Portugal. All these neutral nations refused, except Sweden. It is possible that the motivation for Sweden's acceptance may have been to continue its policy of cooperating or appearing to cooperate with both sides.

 Iver Olsen was dispatched to Sweden to represent the American War Refugee Board in its quest to find a Swedish national to represent them. Olsen was also affiliated with the OAS, which was the predecessor of the CIA. This connection may have later added to Soviet concerns regarding Wallenberg.

Iver Olsen got together a committee of prominent Swedish Jews to advise him on the best means of helping Jews in Hungary, Europe's last remaining Jewish community. Among this group were the World Jewish Congress representative in Stockholm, Norbert Masur, the Swedish Chief Rabbi,

Dr. Marcus Ehrenpreis, and Wallenberg's partner, Kalmon Lauer, an expert on Hungary.

In the final year of World War II, Raoul Wallenberg was recommended to Iver Olsen by Kalmon Lauer to represent the American War Refugee Board. The architect, from the famous, but slightly estranged from family, accepted the challenge.

Why? There is speculation that it was because of a distant relative on Raoul's mother's side who was Jewish. How many people do you know who would volunteer to accept a challenge involving constant danger, and the possibility of death, because of a distant relative he or she didn't know, and had never met? It is probably not many. Rather, it is more likely that Raoul Wallenberg accepted this nearly impossible position, of almost single handedly sparing with the Nazis, to save the lives of those he had never met, because of his compassion. In addition to compassion, he had energy, drive, imagination, was fearless, and, as yet, had no real outlet for his vast creative talents. He is also quoted, in regard to the family banking business, as having said that he did not want to say "no", all day. Mostly, it was his vast compassion for the oppressed, no matter whom, or where, they were.

What Raoul Wallenberg had to offer the American War Refugee Board was his famous name, which was well respected in Europe, his passion, his ability to find simple solutions to complex problems, his unusual grasp of human nature, and his excellent instincts. This was purely a diplomatic position, with no weapons involved. The only 'weapons' Raoul Wallenberg used to accomplish his mission were courage, determination, and imagination.

Raoul was determined not to allow himself to be hamstrung by protocol or tied up by red tape. Fourteen days of intensive negotiations followed on a nine point memorandum drawn up by Wallenberg. It stipulated that (1) he would have a free hand to use any methods he saw fit, including bribery; (2) if the need arose for personal consultations with the Foreign Office, he should be free to return to Stockholm without going through the lengthy procedure of getting permission; (3) if his financial resources proved insufficient, a propaganda campaign would be launched in Sweden to raise more money; (4) he would have adequate status to do the job, so he would be appointed First Secretary of the Swedish legation with a salary of 2,000 crowns a month; (5) he would have the right to contact any persons he wished in Budapest, including avowed enemies of the regime; (6) he would be empowered to deal directly with the Prime Minister or any other member of the Hungarian government without going through the Ambassador; (7) he would be able to send dispatches directly to Stockholm via diplomatic courier, again without using normal channels; (8) he might officially seek an interview with the Regent Miklos Horthy, to ask for his intercession on behalf of the Jews; and (9) he should be authorized to give asylum in buildings belonging to the legation, to persons holding Swedish protective passes.

Wallenberg's demands were so unusual that the matter was referred all the way up to the Prime Minister, who consulted the King before passing down the word, through the Foreign Minister, that Wallenberg's conditions were accepted. By the end of June, Wallenberg was appointed Second Secretary of the Swedish Legation in Budapest.

Herschel V. Johnson, U. S. Minister in Stockholm, cabled Cordell Hull, U. S. Secretary of State, saying: "Olsen and I are of the opinion that the War Refugee Board should be considering ways and means of implementing this action of the Swedish Government, particularly with respect to financial support." Hull cabled back agreeing.

Olsen told Per Anger, of the Swedish Legation in Budapest, who was then in Stockholm, that there would be no problem in continuously putting funds at the disposal of the activities Wallenberg was planning.

"Seldom has a single man been able to accomplish so much from such an impossible starting position, with such small resources, and furthermore, completely lacking any legal ground to stand on" said Lars Berg, a Swedish Diplomat with Raoul Wallenberg in Budapest.

Chapter Four: Hungary

Hungary was partitioned after World War I. Areas in Slovakia and Transylvania were ceded. Thousands who had lost property in the ceded areas, and others from the region, immigrated into central Hungary. In 1929, an uprising led to a Communist regime. This was defeated by a counter revolution led by Regent Miklos Horthy.

Hungary had a hopeless strategic geography located on a plain at the boundary between Eastern and Western Europe. It was open to attack from all sides. In World War II, Hungary was caught between the Allies moving east, and the Axis moving west. Ultimately, Hungary was forced to be allied with the Nazis.

Hungarian Prime Minister Miklos Kallay declared publically on several occasions that Hungary had been forced into the war against its will by the Nazis. The Nazis did not trust Hungary as an ally. Hungary tried to maintain correct relations with the Nazis, baring the way to further Nazi demands. Hungary kept the door open for negotiations with the Allies, primarily the Americans and the British, but it had great anxiety about Russian occupation. Hungarian Authorities dreamed of being able to throw out the Nazis, declare Hungary neutral, and avoid occupation. As a Hungarian patriot, Kallay strove to keep the country intact as long as possible, and as the inevitable showdown that was approaching, hold onto as much of Hungary's resources, territory, and social and political systems, as possible.

The Hungarian authorities, who were tired of the War and Nazi domination, paid little or no attention to the many orders from Berlin to deport Jews. Regent Miklos Horthy, though he had little love for the Jews, could not quite bring himself to allow "his" Jews to be subjected to Hitler's Final Solution – especially since he now believed that his Nazi allies were bound to lose the war. Under Nazi pressure, Hungarians had introduced ordinances primarily intended to reduce the number of Jews in public service, and independent professions, and to limit Jewish activity in commercial, industrial, and banking enterprises.

These ordinances were not enough. There remained approximately 800,000 Jews in the country, and about 250,000 of them were in Budapest. Oberstrumbannfuhrer Adolf Eichmann was instructed by SS Reichsfuhrer Heinrich Himmler to go to Hungary. It was about to be taken over by the Nazis to enforce the total obedience of Regent Horthy, their increasingly reluctant ally. Especially important to the Nazis was Horthy's compliance with the demands for the Final Solution. Eichmann was to organize the concentration and deportation of the Hungarian Jews in the quickest possible time. Eichmann hoped his work in Hungary would earn him a promotion from

Lieutenant Colonel to the rank of full
Colonel.

Hungary was occupied in a single morning
on March 19, 1944. There was a meeting
between Hitler and Horthy. Horthy was
detained against his will. Then "Operation
Margarethe" - the Nazi occupation of
Hungary - took place. The border was
overrun by motorized units. Paratroopers
secured airports and other strategic points.
All official buildings, radio and TV stations,
were quickly occupied by Nazi forces.
Horthy and Kallay were overthrown. The
Hungarian Ambassador to Berlin, General
Sztojay was installed by the Nazis as Prime
Minister. Hungary capitulated that Sunday
morning.

After Horthy was defeated, law and justice
were gone. The Hungarian Nazis, or Arrow
Cross, led by Ferenc Szalasi, seized power.
The Arrow Cross party was made up of
released convicts, drunks, crooks and
sadistic tormentors. Law was a loaded

weapon. The Arrow Cross was more brutal and sadistic than the Nazis. Arrow Cross members had not grown up in the spirit of strict discipline. They had no idea about order, obedience, or proper use of arms.

New recruits to the Arrow Cross were given red and white badges, guns, plenty of ammunition, and no formal discipline. Robber gangs operated independently. Nobody was safe. They shot people who did not get out of their way fast enough. There were no trained leaders or instructors. They plundered everything. Food, wine, and valuables were stolen from the nearest house, regardless of who the owner was.

The most macabre figure in the Arrow Cross was a supposed priest. He dressed in black, and lead a gang. With a crucifix in one hand, and a revolver in the other, he killed every Jew he met on the street.

Unlike the Nazis and Hungarian government, the Arrow Cross knew nothing of diplomatic immunity.

Chapter Five:

Six Months in Budapest

In the six months from July 9, 1944 to January 17, 1945, Raoul Wallenberg is credited with saving 100,000 lives.

Although many people would like to dispute this number, it is accurate. It counts each, and every time a life was saved. Raoul Wallenberg is credited with preventing the destruction of the Budapest ghetto, saving approximately 70,000 lives. Many of these people had also been saved on one or more occasions. Each time a life is saved, it counts. The other approximately 30,000 people were saved by Raoul Wallenberg from deportation trains, death marches, holding areas, rescued from Arrow Cross torture basements, and other life threatening situations.

These are accurate numbers.

When Raoul Wallenberg arrived in
Budapest, the Nazis, led by Adolf
Eichmann, had already wiped out most of
Europe's Jewish communities. The Jews in
the Hungarian countryside were deported at
the rate of 12,000 men, women, and children
daily. By May 1944, 116,000 Hungarian
Jews had perished at Auschwitz. Budapest
was the last remaining Jewish community in
Europe.

Provisional passports, visa certificates, and
Red Cross protection letters were used to
prevent people from being deported.
Wallenberg had a new idea for a more
effective document. It was a so called
Swedish Protective Passport or "Safe Pass".
These were ID papers in blue and yellow
(the Swedish colors), with the three crown
emblem (an official Swedish logo), and a
picture of the bearer. Wallenberg was
trained as an architect, and especially
proficient in design. His impressive looking
Swedish passports replaced the previous

mundane certificates. His passes commanded attention from the Nazis, who were fixated on appearances. Safe passes made the holders feel human again, and gave them hope. These papers had no valid international authority, but Wallenberg was able to obtain a promise from the Hungarian government to recognize several hundred. He issued several thousand.

Wallenberg convinced the other neutral representatives to do the same. The Swiss, Spanish, Portuguese, Turks, and several Latin American countries all participated in his plan. Cardinal Angelo Roncalli, then Apostolic Delegate in Turkey, and later Pope John XXIII, ordered the Papal Nuncio in Budapest, Angelo Rotta, to issue thousands of baptismal certificates, and safe conduct passes. The official Roman Catholic policy in Hungary sought protection for all Jews.

"He (Wallenberg) issued protection passports by the thousands – and saw to it that they were respected. Overnight he rearranged a whole row of apartment buildings into hotels and inspired other neutral legations, and the Church authorities to join at his side. In this way he saved more than one hundred thousand human lives, without exaggeration."

"This heroic deed was achieved in spite of the most active and violent resistance from the otherwise so efficient Gestapo, from the Waffen SS, from the Hungarian government, and from any other number of Nazi and Hungarian authorities."

"The most remarkable thing about Wallenberg's actions, however, was that they were not based on any legal rights whatsoever…Nor was Wallenberg supported by any armed force. Neither weapons nor soldiers gave weight to his words. His only source of power was his unfaltering faith in himself, and the righteousness of his mission."

Lars Berg, Swedish Diplomat in Budapest
with Raoul Wallenberg

Using money from the American War
Refugee Board, Wallenberg set up "safe
houses" - apartment buildings flying the
Swedish flag. These buildings were said to
be temporary housing for those who had
been accepted for residence in Sweden.
Wallenberg set up soup kitchens. He
procured food, medicine, blankets, and other
necessities from contacts he was given by
Kalmon Lauer in Stockholm. He quickly set
up a network of informants, and suppliers of
food and other necessities.

Wallenberg was attached to the Swedish
Legation in Budapest, but had his own
special section. Approximately 400 people,
mostly Jews worked for him. People were
happy to be employed by the Swedish
Legation. The number of Jews being
protected in Swedish houses rose to between
15,000 and 20,000 people. Many other Jews

were helped, or hidden, by the Red Cross, and others.

Before Wallenberg's arrival in Budapest, Eichmann had just completed what he called "a deportation surpassing every preceding deportation in magnitude". He was referring to the Jews in the Hungarian countryside. There remained about 250,000 terrified Jews trapped in the Capital. Eichmann planned to round up the entire Jewish population in Budapest in a stunning 24 hour blitz at the end of July. He hoped to impress Muller and Himmler sufficiently to win a promotion.

Hungarian Regent Horthy instructed the Nazi backed Prime Minister Sztojay that there would be no more deportations. Horthy ordered the Hungarian Nazi Arrow Cross out of the city, leaving Eichmann without manpower.

Instead of a roundup, Eichmann set up a Central Jewish Council to make manipulation of Jews easier. The Council consisted of prominent members of the Jewish community. Eichmann made demands of the Council including around the clock telephone orders from the Gestapo. Jews were instructed by the Nazis to remain calm to avoid a Warsaw-like uprising. Next, Jews were forbidden to leave their homes. They had to give up telephones, radios, cars, and bicycles. Jewish bank accounts were frozen, and food rations reduced. Jews were expelled from civil service and the professions. Jews had to wear a yellow star.

Eichmann needed a location to detain people who had already been rounded up when Horthy suspended deportations. An unused brick factory was taken over for that purpose. It was an open air area, with no sanitary facilities, or protection from the elements. There were 10,000 Jews in an area so small that they were forced to stand up. Young and old people were held there together. Nazis constantly called them

'Pigs'. These unfortunate people were totally demoralized. Individuals were taken aside, and tortured to disclose where they had hidden their valuables. Loud music was played to conceal their screams. Many people died in the brick factory.

Raoul Wallenberg arrived at the brick factory in a diplomatic car with Swedish flags flying. He used a megaphone to demand the release of the "Swedish citizens". He read names from a list. The list of names came from Jews in the brick factory writing their names on scraps of paper, rolling them up, and throwing the papers out when the guards were not looking. Brave Christian children risked their lives playing near the brick factory. They picked up the papers, and through the network of informants, got the names to Wallenberg. In addition, Wallenberg called common names. People took a chance, and came out. His visit made people feel human again, and gave them hope. His "Swedes" were whisked away to safety.

Eventually, more SS troops were sent to Budapest to make up for Horthy's refusal to cooperate. Then the deportations began. Deportation trains usually left in the middle of the night in order to have minimal involvement of the general population. Wallenberg would get word when a deportation train was going to leave through one of his informants. Then he would hurry down with his assistants, often Aryan looking Jews. Wallenberg's assistants went to the other side, and roof of the train. They put Swedish Safe Passes into waiting hands reaching out from the train.

Wallenberg used a loud speaker, and demanded release of "Swedes". The Nazi soldiers at the deportation trains were low ranking Nazis. This was late at night, and the officers were asleep. These young soldiers were afraid to disobey any orders, so they allowed Wallenberg to remove people while they called their officers. People with Swedish Safe Passes came out. Wallenberg asked who had applied for a passport. Since the Nazis could not read Hungarian, people presented anything in their pockets. Wallenberg called these papers "preliminary applications". Wallenberg called out fictitious names. People decided to take a chance, and came out. Then the "Swedes" were put on waiting trucks, and whisked away into the night. By the time the Nazi officers called back, these Jews were gone.

Wallenberg had informants everywhere, and if an action was planned against the Jews, he usually knew about it. Rumors spread of his almost superhuman ability to snatch victims from Nazi executioners.

Death Marches were ordered by Eichmann. The Nazi army was hard pressed by the Russian army. Every piece of rolling stock was needed for military purposes. Russian troops blocked roads east and south. Jews were forced to march west to Austria. Women were in high heels, and men had no overcoats. These poor souls were driven on a 125 mile long march to the Austrian Hungarian border. It took more than a week in winter cold and snow, with no food or shelter. The dead were left on the side of the road. Wallenberg followed the death marches. He brought food, medicine, and blankets. He was able to bring many people back.

The Nazi backed Foreign Minister Baron Gabor Kemeny had a young, attractive wife, whom he loved very much. Baroness Kemeny was an Italian citizen married to the Arrow Cross Foreign Minister. While she was a young student in boarding school, she became friendly with a Hungarian classmate. She was invited for a vacation in Hungary by her friend. During this visit, the beautiful young Italian met Baron Kemeny. They fell in love. Her family approved of the marriage because of his title. After their marriage, it became evident that it was a title only, and there was no money involved. Baroness Kemeny had to get a job! Her employer was in Wallenberg's network of informants, and introduced the Baroness to Raoul Wallenberg. After that, when all else failed, Wallenberg would ask the Baroness. She, in turn, would ask her husband. Baroness Kemeny would threaten to return to her parents in Italy if he refused. Afraid of losing his wife, the Hungarian Nazi Foreign Minister never refused anything. He agreed to all Wallenberg's demands.

The Arrow Cross, aka Hungarian Gendarmes, aka Hungarian Nazis, were violent, usually drunk individuals, who made horrible acts of torture and murder common in Budapest. They brought Jews into basements used for torture. There, Jews were forced to do such bizarre things as clean toilets by licking them with their tongues. Many people died in these torture basements. Informants told Wallenberg where they were located, and when Jews were in there. Unarmed, Wallenberg entered, and removed victims, by confronting the thugs. Another horrific scene in Budapest was at the Danube River. Arrow Cross gangsters tied three Jews together, and pushed them into the river. Then they shot the middle person. This pulled down the other two causing them to drown. Wallenberg had divers hidden on the shore, who rescued as many people as possible.

Often Wallenberg appeared when the Arrow Cross was rounding up Jews. He announced in a loud voice in German that he had orders to take these Jews. Then he left with them before the startled Arrow Cross knew what was happening. He was the driving force behind agreements entered into with the Arrow Cross regime concerning their respecting not only Swedish protective passports, but also corresponding documents of other neutral nations. Raoul Wallenberg bribed Arrow Cross officials, threatened executions, and promised pardons after the arrival of the Russians. He became hated, and feared, by the Arrow Cross.

Wallenberg was Eichmann's special enemy. Eichmann was especially interested in stopping Wallenberg. He expressed his intention to have the "Jew Dog Wallenberg" shot. Since the Nazis needed their relationship with the Swedish Government, attacking a Swedish Diplomat would not have been acceptable. Instead of a direct attack, attempts were made to run Wallenberg's car off the road to look like an accident. As a precaution, Wallenberg slept in a different place each night, and usually only slept for about four hours. Himmler wanted to insure good Nazi – Swedish relations, and ordered Eichmann to respect members of the Swedish Legation.

Wallenberg invited Eichmann to dinner to confront him. Eichmann was from a lower social class than the famous Wallenberg's, so he was delighted. Wallenberg completely forgot about it, and found Eichmann waiting for him in the Legation. Many of the Hungarian citizens who had left Budapest, as well as the foreign Embassies that had been evacuated, had left their belongings to the Swedes for safe keeping. Wallenberg called Lars Berg who was staying in a Count's charming and comfortable house in Buda, a section of Budapest. The house had six servants, including a wonderful cook. They prepared the most sumptuous dinner, complete with the Count's fine porcelain and silver. At the end of dinner, Wallenberg pulled back a curtain showing Eichmann the lights from Russian artillery in the distance. It was clear that the end was very near.

The remaining 70,000 Jews were forced to stay in a ghetto which was scheduled to be destroyed in a manner similar to the Warsaw ghetto. Raoul Wallenberg found out that General Schmidthuber was the Nazi commander who was to give the order to destroy the ghetto. Wallenberg threatened General Schmidthuber that if he gave the order, Wallenberg would personally see that Schmidthuber was tried as a war criminal. The order was never given.

Then the Russians arrived.

Chapter Six:
The Disappearance

The Russian army liberated, or occupied, Budapest in January 1945.

By that time, Raoul Wallenberg had personally saved 30,000 people from train deportations, death marches, and the Arrow Cross. In addition, he saved the 70,000 residents of the Budapest ghetto, bringing the total to 100,000 lives saved during six months. The only weapons he used were courage, determination, and imagination.

Raoul Wallenberg was taken into Russian "protective custody" on January 17, 1945.

During the occupation of Budapest, Joseph Stalin ordered the Russians to conduct house to house searches. All diplomats were taken into "protective custody", and sent to Moscow. In Moscow, they went into the infamous Lubyanka Prison, and entered the Gulag Archipelago.

In the late 1940's and early 1950's diplomats returned to their countries. Maj Von Dardle waited as the ships arrived in Stockholm. But Raoul was never on them.

Maj never stopped doing everything humanly possible to find her son, Raoul. Nothing worked. Then in 1979, when she left this world, there was an imperceptible, but real shift in the cosmos. Things started happening. Eventually by 1988, everything started to change when a candle light vigil was held by a handful of people outside the Soviet Mission in Glen Cove, New York.

Part Two –
The Search

Chapter Seven:
Werbell's Article

Wallenberg is my last name. Growing up, I was told about the famous Wallenberg family in Sweden where my grandparents came from. I did not feel any connection to them since they were rich and famous, and we were anything but that. Additionally, they were experts at business, and I felt more inclined to be idealistic. They meant nothing to me. When I was in my 20's, my entire family of origin left this world. First it was my mother, Mary, then my father's sister, aunt Edith, and finally my father, John. It was all within the span of two and a half years. I was pregnant with my second child, Marisa, when my mother died. At the end, I was left with two small daughters, Becky and Marisa, in a crumbling marriage which soon ended.

At that point, I became curious about that 'famous family in Sweden', and I decided to do some research. I discovered that they were indeed rich and famous, very astute in business, and that one was a 'War Hero'. I assumed that the 'War Hero' had gone to Great Britain, joined the RAF, and shot down Nazi fighter planes. I was not impressed. That was in the late 1970's.

By 1980, I had collected a very modest inheritance. I started looking for a small, affordable house in Long Island. My friend, Merrell was kind enough to bring me the Sunday New York Times every week so I could look in the Real Estate section.

On Sunday, March 30, 1980, the New York Times magazine had a cover article on Raoul Wallenberg which trailed for pages. My life was forever changed! I was nearly hysterical to learn that a man who saved 100,000 people was missing, and no one was trying to find him. I didn't know it then, but a more than a decade long odyssey was about to begin when I read Frederick Werbell and Eleanor Lester's New York Times magazine article.

Chapter Eight:
The Early Years

I found a small, affordable house in Sea Cliff. Previously, I had gone to Sea Cliff with my friend, Hildy, to see the Fourth of July fireworks. I fell in love with the view of Hempstead Harbor from Prospect Park at the end of Sea Cliff Avenue. It reminded me of Portugal, where I had spent time years earlier. The house was a "fixer upper", or "handyman special", but I did not know that then. In fact, I didn't know anything about home ownership. I was the first one in my immediate family to buy a house. And I did it alone, and with two small children.

The house was over 100 years old. It was built on a former tent site. Sea Cliff was originally a Methodist camp ground for people who came there on ferries or steamboats from New York City for summer vacations. Eventually, people bought their own tent sites, and later built small summer cottages on them. Throughout the years, these cottages were winterized, added on to, and added on to. Nothing matched, which people thought was 'charming'. The property was no longer a 'tent site', but a "non-conforming lot". The house bordered on the property line on one side, and it was a few inches from the property line on the other side. But, it was affordable, and Sea Cliff was beautiful!

We moved in during January 1981, in the dead of winter, to a house with no insulation. The snow gathered *inside* the windows! During the day, my two young daughters and I wore blankets over our clothes. At night, when they were sleeping, I cried.

The house did not have a refrigerator, so I put the food outside the kitchen window. It was definitely cold outside. In the morning I would get up before my daughters, and go to the store to buy fresh milk for their breakfast before they went to school. I have since stopped all dairy and I use only plant milk – soy or almond. Eventually I applied for a credit card. There were complications which delayed the process. Finally, I bought a refrigerator on credit.

Eventually, spring came to the little house in Sea Cliff, and with the crocuses and daffodils, came a job in Manhasset. Bob Gustafson, a man of Swedish descent, hired me. The job was in sales. For motivation we had to discuss what we would do when we earned our commissions. Others dreamed of new cars, vacations, clothes, jewelry, etc. My dream was plumbing fixtures. Casual conversations in the office revolved around personal issues. Mine were about house painting - inside and outside.

Bob was a good friend. He helped me in my sales career, which neither one of us was really very good at. He also worked on my house getting it into minimal livable condition. We shared a deep concern about the missing Wallenberg.

The Raoul Wallenberg Committee of the United States was forming in Manhattan. Bob and I started attending their functions together. It was initially run by the daughter of the physician to the King of Sweden, Lena Biorck Kaplan. Later, it was run by her neighbor, Rachael Oestraicher Haspel. Other active members were Rabbi Bruce Cole, Vice President, Betty Throne-Holst, Program Chairman, Alan C. Greenberg, Chairman of the Executive Board. Through these Committee meetings, demonstrations, and black tie fund raiser dinners at the Waldorf Astoria, I met Elie Wiesel, authors Frederick Werbell and Eleanor Lester, dignitaries, survivors, nobility, and other people interested in starting Wallenberg Committees. One thing I did not see was anything being done to find the missing Wallenberg.

At one of the meetings in Manhattan, I met an elderly couple who had been saved by Wallenberg. They seemed agitated. It was as if there were some strong unfulfilled need that was driving them. They knew that my last name was Wallenberg. It seemed that they had been carrying a burden for years. It was the need to say, "Thank you". They said it to me. I guess if you couldn't find the Wallenberg you want, you make do with the one you have. I could sense this very deep need. I did everything I could to try to channel the spirit of Raoul Wallenberg, which was a first for me. Somewhere, from deep inside, from some other place, I produced, "You're welcome". The relief on their faces was worth a million dollars! For the first time in my life I was living in two worlds. I was just grateful that if I was called to do, or be, something extraordinary, at least it wasn't dangerous like it was for the World War II heroes.

Another survivor I met was Susan Tabor. I even visited her in her apartment in Stuyvesanttown, Manhattan. The first time I met her, I was immediately struck by what a lovely, gentle woman she was. It was mindboggling to me that anyone ever would have wanted to murder her!

Other people interested in starting Wallenberg Committees included Norma Anderson from Upstate New York. I met Norma at a fund raiser dinner at the Waldorf Astoria. I helped her found her Committee by arranging for Eleanor Lester, the author, and Susan Tabor, the survivor, to speak at Norma's meeting in Jamestown, New York.

Agnes Adachi, a survivor and member of Wallenberg's staff in Budapest, founded a Wallenberg Committee in Queens, New York. Leona Feldman from Philadelphia, Pennsylvania, founded a Wallenberg Committee there. I founded the Raoul Wallenberg Committee of Long Island.

In October 1981, Hungarian born Congressman Tom Lantos from California introduced a Resolution which made Raoul Wallenberg an Honorary American Citizen. Everyone was happy. Congressman Lantos' wife, Annette, had a family member who was saved by Raoul Wallenberg. President Regan signed the bill into law. Again, nothing happened to find Wallenberg.

I began to read everything I could find on Raoul Wallenberg. By that time there was a plethora of books on him. I continued to attend all meetings, fund raisers, and demonstrations by the Raoul Wallenberg Committee of the United States in Manhattan. I began to give talks wherever I could to create awareness of this hero, and his plight. I reached out to Elie Wisel and others. There was still no Raoul.

Chapter Nine:
The Demonstration

On January 17, 1988, a demonstration was held outside the Soviet residence on Dosoris Lane, Glen Cove, New York, to seek the release of the prison records of Raoul Wallenberg.

Until that time, I thought of myself as a Long Island housewife / mother. I did not feel I had the background, skills, or experience to accomplish anything on the international level. However, I had run out of patience with those who did seem to have those qualifications. They did not actually accomplish anything important - namely, finding Raoul Wallenberg.

The idea came from a tiny article in the back of Newsday, a Long Island newspaper. The article was about United States officials being banned from a Soviet controlled beach on the other side of the world. This was in response to the City of Glen Cove banning Soviet officials from using the Glen Cove beach.

The Glen Cove ban was a purely financial decision. The Soviet diplomats from the United Nations in New York have a weekend / summer residence in Glen Cove. In order for them to use the local beach, the City of Glen Cove must provide security. This is a somewhat complicated, and expensive proposition.

Funds for security came out of the City budget. There were more City Councilmen voting against this use of funds, then voting for it. As a result, the Soviets were not allowed to use the beach. It was nothing personal.

As retaliation, American diplomats were not allowed to use a Soviet controlled beach somewhere on the other side of the world. Sea Cliff, where I lived, is an enclave of

Glen Cove. I realized immediately that world events could be influenced right here.

I decided to hold a candlelight vigil in front of the Soviet Mission on Dosoris Lane in Glen Cove on January 17, 1988, the 43rd anniversary of Raoul Wallenberg's imprisonment by Soviet authorities.

The purpose of the vigil was to focus public attention on the fate of Raoul Wallenberg, the Swedish Diplomat, credited with saving 100,000 lives in Budapest during World War II on behalf of President Roosevelt's American War Refugee Board with American tax payer dollars.

Also, it was to press for the release of his prison records from the Soviets. Raoul Wallenberg was made an honorary American citizen by an act of Congress in 1981, and had been imprisoned by the Soviets since their liberation of Budapest in 1945.

He had been sighted in Soviet prisons many times since then, followed by mysterious deaths of witnesses. Sightings had been confirmed by Amnesty International as late as the 1980's.

In everything I had read, and all the meetings I had attended, the only thing that made any sense to me was a statement by Andrei Sakharov which said:

 "For about ten years now I have known about the tragic fate of Raoul Wallenberg. I consider him to be one of those people of the 20th century to whom all of mankind is greatly indebted and ought to be proud of. I believe the organization of an International Hearing on his case, and an international defense campaign on his behalf are very important.

Ever since I learned about him, I have thought a great deal as to possible ways of searching for him. I have spoken with many different kinds of people who at one time or another have passed through Soviet prisons and labor camps, but I have never once succeeded in meeting anyone who could tell me anything about Raoul Wallenberg's fate. Now it seems important to me (although I am not putting too much hope in this) that the Soviet authorities be forced to transfer Raoul Wallenberg's investigation file and his personal prison or labor camp records to the Wallenberg Defense Committee.

Since the Soviet authorities have officially admitted that Wallenberg was arrested and was imprisoned in the USSR then such files must exist (and they are kept forever). It is possible that an investigation file, as well as personal prison or labor camp records will help to shed light on when Raoul Wallenberg was imprisoned and in which prisons or labor camps he was confined.

That would make it possible to search for testifiers and eye witnesses precisely from these places of imprisonment.

I realize that it is extremely difficult to obtain any kind of documents from the

Soviet authorities but this should be attempted. At the same time, the refusal of the Soviet authorities to release Wallenberg's files would testify to the fact that they have something to hide.

Thus, I believe that the release of Wallenberg's files is the minimum cooperative effort in which the Swedish Government and the Swedish and international community can partake and have every right to demand from the Soviet authorities."

Andrei Sakharov, March 21, 1981 Gorky, USSR

It seemed to me that this was the easiest, and most sensible, first step in the effort to seek the release of Raoul Wallenberg from Soviet custody. It was the easiest for the Soviets, and therefore most likely to lead the way to the eventually resolving the mystery of Raoul Wallenberg's disappearance.

I followed all the proper protocols, and requested permission from Glen Cove Police Chief Timothy Edwards to hold the candlelight vigil across from Killenworth, the Soviet residence in Glen Cove.

I explained that the purpose of the vigil was to protest the fate of Raoul Wallenberg who was taken into Soviet custody at the end of World War II after saving 100,000 lives from Nazi extermination in Budapest while representing President Roosevelt's War Refugee Board. Reliable sources had confirmed that Mr. Wallenberg has been alive in Soviet prisons for all these years. The vigil was to be entirely peaceful, and include saying prayers and singing hymns, specifically "Amazing Grace" and "How Great Thou Art".

Permission was granted by Chief Edwards on December 4, 1987.

There was not much to work with! Milton Sutton, retired Public Relations professional, and a member of my Amnesty International Group 17 in Great Neck, taught me the five W's of writing a press release. Who, What, When, Where and Why should all appear in the first sentence of a press release. I wrote press releases, and mailed them to the local media: Newsday, Anton Community Papers, News Channel 12, and the New York Times.

I invited Elected Officials: my Congressman: Congressman Robert Mrazek, my Senators: Senator Daniel Patrick Moynihan and Senator Alfonse D'Amato. I explained who Raoul Wallenberg was, why this date was important, that there would be press coverage during the vigil, and coffee and cake afterwards.

I further requested a Representative or Staff Member to say a few words for them at the vigil. I also invited Elie Wiesel, and several Rabbis and other Clergymen from Long Island where I had given presentations on Raoul Wallenberg.

Senator Moynihan and Congressman Mrazek sent beautifully worded, lovely declinations. Congressman Mrazek promised to send a Staff Member. Almost everyone else was supportive, but unable to attend.

The Peace and Justice Committee of my church, Saint Boniface, Martyr, in Sea Cliff provided my fellow demonstrators. Eisenstadt's, the local Department store in Glen Cove, had left over Hanukkah candles on sale, which I purchased for the Demonstration. I even wrote to the Soviet Mission, and explained what was being done, and why.

The Demonstration was held on January 17, 1988 by me and other members of the Saint Boniface Peace and Justice Committee. We stood in the cold and slush, on Dosoris Lane outside the entrance to the High School. We were across the street from the Soviet Mission with our matches and discount priced leftover Hanukkah candles. There was no formal program. It was just a small group of unspectacular local residents. But we were joined by the Mayor of Glen Cove, Donald DeRiggi, and Glen Cove City Councilman Steve Gonzalez!

The vigil appeared on Long Island Cable TV News 12, and was covered by the Glen Cove Record Pilot. Congressman Bob Mrazek was represented by Robert Zimmerman. Many members of the Jewish community and the general public attended, in addition to the Saint Boniface Peace and Justice Committee.

After the vigil, I sent out thank you letters to the elected officials who participated, and a follow up press release explaining that on January 17, 1945 Raoul Wallenberg had been taken into Soviet custody during their liberation of Budapest. Evidence of his imprisonment proliferated followed by mysterious deaths of witnesses. Amnesty International confirmed that Wallenberg was alive in Soviet prison.

I initiated a letter writing campaign at the vigil, to Soviet Secretary General Mikhail Gorbachev, and President Ronald Regan. It appeared in the local press article about the vigil, and all were invited to participate. Glen Cove Mayor Donald DiRiggi sent a letter to the Soviet Ambassador to the United Nations requesting information on the whereabouts of Raoul Wallenberg. The Ambassador had previously contacted Mayor DiRiggi several times regarding other matters. At that time, Wallenberg was said to be alive in prison only a few months earlier, according to his half-brother in Stockholm.

I sent thank you letters to Glen Cove Mayor Donald DiRiggi, who had attended, and to Congressman Bob Mrazek for sending Robert Zimmerman to represent him. I enclosed a recent article giving evidence that Wallenberg, who was a victim of terrible injustice, was alive in Soviet prisons for 43 years, and expressed my intention to continue holding demonstrations at the Soviet Mission. In addition, I sent thank you letters to donors, Arthur Michaelson, Milton and Freema Sutton, from my Great Neck Amnesty International Group 17, and to Rev. James Christ, at whose congregation I had given a presentation on Wallenberg, in appreciation for their generous donations. I enclosed copies of publications pointing out that reliable sources confirm that Raoul Wallenberg was alive in a Soviet prison as recently as a few months earlier.

Graciously, Bob Mrazek wrote back saying, "I just wanted to thank you for your note of January 26th, as well as to congratulate you for the wonderful work you are doing in regard to the release of Raoul Wallenberg. I only wish we were as successful in getting a full accounting on Mr. Wallenberg…I look forward to working with you in the future…"

In another letter, Bob said "In this vast slaughterhouse of a world that we live in, it is a privilege for me to represent caring, concerned people like yourself."

Chapter Ten:
Why Legislation?

Encouraged by the modest success of the first Demonstration, I decided to plan a series of ongoing Demonstrations. The intention was to continue demonstrating until the Soviets freed the missing Wallenberg.

It made sense to hold the Demonstrations on days which were meaningful to the cause of Raoul Wallenberg. These were on, or close to January 17, his last day of freedom, August 4, his birthday, and October 5, for Honorary Citizen Day.

The next demonstration was a Birthday Demonstration planned for August. As usual, permission was requested from Glen Cove Police Chief Timothy Edwards. This time I gave him a book on Raoul Wallenberg. Press releases and invitations were sent out. What made this

Demonstration especially fortuitous was that I purchased a birthday sheet cake from Hubie's, a local bakery in Glen Head.

News Channel 12 attended the Demonstration, as well as the Glen Cove Record Pilot, the Great Neck Record, where my Amnesty International Group was located, and the Long Island Catholic, because there was no school news in August. Carol Siegel, a Glen Cove resident and loyal supporter from the American Jewish Congress, was delighted to appear in the Long Island Catholic. It was a first for her!

More importantly, Hubie was excited to see his cake on TV. Next time I saw him, he asked me why I didn't tell him that his cake would be on TV. I had no way of knowing that in advance. Hubie gave me free cakes for my Demonstrations from then on. I was making progress!

Next, I planned a Demonstration for Honorary American Citizen Day in October.

I decided to expand my base of support by inviting all the local elected officials in Nassau County. Bob Burnhart, of my Amnesty International Group 17, gave me a list of them from the League of Women Voters.

I wrote a hand written invitation which read something like, "Dear Elected Official, You are cordially invited to attend a peaceful Demonstration on behalf of Raoul Wallenberg…" This was photocopied, and mailed to all the Nassau County elected officials listed by the League of Women Voters. These had to be the least prestigious invitations ever sent. I received back many, many lovely declinations, and some acceptances!

In addition, I wrote to Soviet Ambassador Alexander Belonogov, at the Soviet Mission in Glen Cove, to inform him of the planned Demonstration on behalf of Raoul Wallenberg. It said in part,

"On October 5, 1981 an act of Congress signed by the President of the United States made Raoul Wallenberg an Honorary American Citizen. We the people of this area of Nassau County, Long Island express our outrage at the kidnap and detention of Raoul Wallenberg, Honorary American Citizen. Further, we protest his continued imprisonment and demand his immediate release. On Sunday, October 2 at 7:00 P.M. there will be a peaceful demonstration in front of your mission on Dosoris Lane on behalf of Raoul Wallenberg, Honorary American Citizen.

Sharon L. Wallenberg, President,
Raoul Wallenberg Committee of Long Island."

By this time, I had started to formulate a program to go with the Demonstration. I thought adding an expert on Wallenberg would be a nice touch, so I invited Rabbi Werbell to join us. Realizing that I needed to make the invitation enticing to attract a celebrity author, I offered transportation, dinner, and an honorarium.

The transportation was me driving into Manhattan, and picking him up. Dinner was a Pot Luck thanks to my friends and supporters. I left my front door unlocked when I went to Manhattan. When I got back with Frederick Werbell, the guests had arrived with the food, set the table, and had a sumptuous meal ready. Rabbi Werbell and I formed a friendship, and he continued to attend my many events – even without the transportation, dinner, and honorarium.

After dinner, we all headed out to Dosoris Lane for the early evening Demonstration. It was just before the elections, so there was a nice turnout of Elected Officials. It felt like there were more Elected Officials than private citizens standing in front of the entrance to the High School, across the street from the Soviet Mission. I met District Attorney Denis Dillon, who became a lifelong friend; County Executive Thomas

Gulotta, one of the classiest people I have ever met; Assemblyman Lewis Yevoli, who later became County Executive; and Assemblyman Thomas P. DiNapoli, currently New York State Comptroller, who became my next greatest supporter.

The heroic accomplishments of Mr. Wallenberg, as well as his tragic fate in Soviet captivity since 1945, were spoken about by elected officials of both parties. District Attorney Denis Dillon gave an eloquent commentary. Other equally impressive speakers included Assemblymen Thomas DiNapoli and Lewis Yevoli, Glen Cove Deputy Mayor Anna Iverson, representing Mayor Donald DiRiggi, and City Councilman Steve Gonzales. Candidates for office Robert Zimmerman and Joe Cavello also participated.

A letter from Congressman Bob Mrazek was read which said:

"Please excuse my absence tonight and accept my best wishes to all those attending this important vigil.

There are many reasons to keep the name of Raoul Wallenberg alive. The great humanitarian deeds of Mr. Wallenberg need no amplification. His efforts to save over 100,000 Jews during World War II remain as a shining example of humanity during one of the darkest periods of history. It is essential that the government of the United States continue to make every effort on behalf of this unique man.

The name of Raoul Wallenberg also serves as a symbol of hope for future generations. Young people who study the life of Raoul Wallenberg can only be inspired to work for a better world. For this reason, I hope that the Raoul Wallenberg Committee of Long Island will continue to pursue its worthwhile commitment to keep his memory alive.

Once again, please accept my best wishes and prayers on this occasion."

Rabbi Frederick Werbell, author of "Lost Hero" – the basis for the Richard Chamberlain television movie on Raoul Wallenberg, gave some background information. Werbell sited specific incidents proving Raoul Wallenberg was alive in a Soviet prison. He also encouraged the crowd by saying gatherings such as these are very helpful in securing the release of Raoul Wallenberg.

At my request, a letter writing campaign to the Soviet Ambassador to request the release of the prison records of Raoul Wallenberg, was started, and continued at all future demonstrations. I mentioned that the New York Times carries stories almost daily of Raoul Wallenberg still being alive in Soviet prison. Nassau County officials began the tedious task of trying to secure information from the Soviet Union.

The Demonstration was lovely. County Executive Thomas Gulotta graciously presented me with a Proclamation officially making October 5 Raoul Wallenberg Honorary Citizen Day in Nassau County.

The demonstration was conducted as daylight faded, and evening began. The autumn weather was crisp and pleasant. After the Demonstration, we all returned to our cars. As soon as I heard the last car door shut, it began to rain. It was almost as if even the Almighty was cooperating, and supporting the movement.

Naturally, I followed through with thank you letters to everyone. Elie Wisel wrote many letters to me, and expressed the need to see the Soviet records. Many others wrote back, including Assemblyman Thomas DiNapoli. In addition, he enclosed a copy of his letter to Ambassador Belonogov, which read in part

"Many of us in this country are concerned about the whereabouts of honorary American Citizen, Raoul Wallenberg. Since his disappearance at the end of World War II there have been many pieces of evidence that strongly suggest that Mr. Wallenberg may not be deceased, as has been officially reported.

In the interest of resolving this matter once and for all and in the spirit of glasnost which Mr. Gorbachev has fostered, I hereby request that the prison records relating to the Wallenberg case be released by your government. Your favorable response to this request would be most welcome by myself and millions of New Yorkers."

Tom's letter to me suggested I contact him, which I did. A meeting was set up in his Great Neck office. My concern was that I would not recognize him, since it was getting dark outside when I met him. There was no problem with that. He was the only one in the office when I was shown in. He said "I am going to introduce legislation to seek the release of Raoul Wallenberg's prison records.

All I could think of was "Why legislation?"

Chapter Eleven:

It's Time To Meet The Soviets

Legislation is a law introduced and passed in the State Legislature, or on the Federal level in Congress in Washington. Since there is no way to make a law which is binding on another country, it is replaced by a Legislative Resolution. This means it is a nonbinding expression of the wishes of a majority of Legislators.

A Legislative Staffer in Assemblyman Tom DiNapoli's office wrote a draft, which I reviewed. I added information which I thought was relevant, and changed details that I felt could be more accurate. Some of it was questionable to me. The Staffer just pleasantly told me we would leave that out. It was very easy. I contacted New York

State Senator Norman Levy, of Long Island, to sponsor the Senate version, which he did.

While Tom was busy in Albany, I organized the January Demonstration. I again requested permission from Glen Cove Police Chief Timothy Edwards, who was becoming my pen pal. I invited him to join us for cake afterwards, which he never did. Hubie graciously contributed a sheet cake for the get together after the Demonstration at Saint Paul's Church, Highland Avenue, Glen Cove. I invited Elected Officials, Elie Wiesel, who had become another pen pal, and this time Lars Berg, a Swedish Diplomat who had been with Wallenberg in Budapest.

I wrote a lovely letter to Soviet Ambassador Alexander Belonogov, resident of Killenworth, the Soviet Mission in Glen Cove, notifying him of the Demonstration. It mentioned that all elected officials in Nassau and Suffolk Counties, Long Island, had been invited. Further, it stated that a Resolution had been introduced in the New

York State Legislature demanding the release of the prison records of Raoul Wallenberg. The same Resolution would be introduced in the United States House of Representatives by Congressman Robert Mrazek. In the spirit of Glasnost, I cordially invited him and his colleagues to join us and also have coffee and cake afterwards.

By now there was always a program. This involved Speakers and everyone signing a Petition to the Soviet Ambassador. I also asked Elected Officials to write to the Soviet Ambassador, and many did. Among them was County Executive Thomas Gulotta, who stated in part:

"I urge you to release all prison records relative to Raoul Wallenberg...As a concerned United States citizen, I ask you to arrange for the production of the prison records of Mr. Wallenberg to the 'Raoul Wallenberg Committee of Long Island.' Since the Soviet Union has indicated that Raoul Wallenberg died of natural causes in prison, I can see no difficulty in complying with this request. I believe that the release of these records will go a long way toward resolving this issue."

New York State Assemblyman, (later Nassau County Executive) Lewis Yevoli wrote:

"I join at this time with many other officials in demanding that the Soviet Union release the prison records of Raoul Wallenberg, a diplomat of Sweden taken prisoner by Soviet troops in Budapest, Hungary on January 17, 1945.

Mr. Wallenberg is known in history as 'The Angel of Rescue' in his successful efforts to save thousands of then surviving Hungarian Jews from the gas chambers of Auschwitz. By issuing thousands of protective passes, he set up safe houses for targeted Jews pursued by the Nazi officials of occupied Hungary and is credited with preventing German forces from blowing up the Budapest ghetto with 70,000 inhabitants.

On January 17, 1945, during the Soviet liberation of Budapest, Raoul Wallenberg was taken into Soviet captivity. The Russian government insists that Mr. Wallenberg died in prison in1947, but no documents have been produced, nobody ever returned, and no specific date of death announced. There are continuing stories that Raoul Wallenberg may still be alive in a Soviet prison.

I am taking this opportunity, Ambassador Belonogov, to demand that Mr. Wallenberg's prison records be released to the United States Government. Raoul Wallenberg was granted honorary American citizenship for his courage, imagination and valor. It is time the Soviet Government give us the full details on both the imprisonment and present status of one of World war Two's legitimate heroes.

Sincerely, Lewis Yevoli
Member, New York State Assembly"

New York State Assemblyman Philip Healy wrote in part:

"I have been informed that he (Raoul Wallenberg) was taken into the Soviet Union in 1945. The Soviet government states that he died in prison in 1947. No documents have ever been provided, nor any body recovered.

I urge you to release the prison records of Mr. Wallenberg to interested parties so that this matter can be solved."

Glen Cove City Councilman Steve Gonzales wrote,

"I believe freedom-loving peoples everywhere must continue to press for the release of the prison records of Raoul Wallenberg. It is important that interested persons…not let up in the quest to have the real facts behind the imprisonment of Mr. Wallenberg revealed."

Author, Wallenberg Expert, and Swedish
Rabbi, Frederick Werbell attended the
Demonstration to remember the anniversary
of the disappearance of Raoul Wallenberg
into Soviet captivity. Also attending were
Nassau County District Attorney Denis
Dillon, Assemblyman Thomas P. DiNapoli,
Glen Cove Mayor Donald De Riggi, Glen
Cove City Councilman Steve Gonzalez,
representatives of Congressman Robert
Mrazek, County Executive Thomas Gulotta,
New York State Senator Norman Levy, (Co-
sponsor of the Wallenberg Resolution in
Albany), Carol and Jeff Seigel from the
American Jewish Congress with their new
baby, supporters from Glen Cove, Sea Cliff,
and the general public. Congressmen
Thomas Downey and Norman Lent, and
New York State Senator Frank Padavan
thanked me for the invitation, saying that
they had prior commitments, and asked to be
kept informed of progress.

By that time, I had come up with an additional idea to keep the momentum going. It was to build a statue of Raoul Wallenberg on Long Island. George Gach, a personal friend, and sculptor from Roslyn, made a miniature copy of a statue of Raoul Wallenberg in Hungary as an example of what we could do. It is visible in photos of the Demonstration.

The Demonstration was held on January 15. It included reading a letter from Congressman Robert Mrazek which said in part,

"I am most proud of your committee's relentless efforts on behalf of a great humanitarian, Raoul Wallenberg. It is important that this cause be kept before the people of Long Island and our nation."

In the crowd of onlookers at the Demonstration, I saw a photographer. When I was able to slip away, I approached him, and discovered that he was a freelance photographer who sold his photos to Newsday, the Long Island Newspaper. That is how I met Steve Berman. From then on, he was always invited to all my events.

Two days later on January 17, Assemblyman Thomas DiNapoli's and State Senator Norman Levy's Raoul Wallenberg Legislative Resolution passed the New York State Legislature in Albany. Tom timed its passing to coincide with the actual date of Raoul Wallenberg's disappearance. Nice touch! Thank you, Tom!

The momentum of this cause was starting to accelerate in Long Island. However, as impressive as this was, it still did nothing to secure the release of Raoul Wallenberg.

What good is all this without Soviet involvement? I decided that we should take our Legislative Resolutions, and present it to the Soviets at the United Nations. I suggested this to Tom. He said "No, we can't do that. We need to make an appointment."

It was time to meet the Soviets!

Chapter Twelve:

I'm Coming Back With My Congressman

The job of making an appointment with the Soviets fell to Assemblyman Tom DiNapoli's Executive Assistant, Phyllis Joseph. Phyllis worked very hard at this. I actually felt sorry for her. She put so much heart and soul into a seemingly hopeless situation.

The first step was to contact the State Department because it was mistakenly assumed that they would actually care about someone who worked on behalf of the American War Refugee Board with American tax payer dollars. Wrong. It was the official policy of the United States State Department not to interfere in internal affairs of foreign governments. That included the unjust incarceration of Raoul Wallenberg.

We were not deterred. Disappointed, even bitterly disappointed on my part perhaps, but not deterred. We finally took matters into our own hands, and Phyllis called the Soviet Mission in Manhattan.

They were delighted to hear from us, and anxious to meet us! Yes, sometimes in life you hit things just right. Gorbachov had initiated Glasnost and Perestroika due to internal Soviet economic problems. The Soviets were anxious to build bridges with economically successful countries in the hope of bettering their own situation. They saw this as that opportunity. We were oblivious… lucky, but oblivious.

In Phyllis Joseph's own words:

"I am happy to share with you the recollection I have regarding the arrangements made by this office for the appointment at the Soviet Mission.

According to my log, I made the first call to the Mission on January 18, 1998. The person that I spoke to is: Sergei Shestakov who accepted my call on behalf of Ambassador Alexander Belonogov with whom I was trying to make the appointment. Mr. Shestakov was most cordial and helpful. He said he would get back to me regarding the possibility of the meeting, time, and place. Several phone calls later, it was confirmed that the meeting would take place at the Soviet Mission, 36 East 67th Street, on Thursday, January 26th at 3:00 pm with Dmitri Bykov, Deputy Permanent Representative.

The Assemblyman, yourself, Rabbi Werbell, and I were welcomed to the Mission by Vadim I. Lukyanovich, L.L.D. Counsellor (Legal Affairs)."

Tom had suggested to me that I invite Rabbi Werbel, which I did. I suggested to Tom that we bring Phyllis as a justly earned opportunity to participate in the fruits of her labors.

On January 26, 1989, Assemblyman Thomas P. DiNapoli, Rabbi Frederick Werbell, and Executive Assistant Phyllis Joseph accompanied Raoul Wallenberg Committee of Long Island Chairwoman Sharon Wallenberg to present a Legislative Resolution calling for the release of the prison records of Raoul Wallenberg to the Soviet Officials at the United Nations in New York.

At this point in time, or possibly earlier, I realized I was in over my head. I knew I needed help beyond myself, and made Creator God, Higher Power, Infinite Wisdom, Loving Kindness an integral part of the equation. I fasted for two days before the Soviet meeting. Then on the day of the meeting I ate normally. After that, whenever there was an important event, I fasted for two days prior to it for Divine Assistance.

We were very cordially welcomed by the Soviet officials, Demetri Bykov (who later became a personal friend), and Vadim

Lukyanovich. They couldn't have been more congenial, or more perfectly charming hosts. We were offered a choice of drinks, as well as something light to eat. It was lovely.

The only thing we didn't do was succeed in was getting the conversation to focus on Raoul Wallenberg. That seemed impossible. Added to that frustration were Werbell's constant attempts to secure Soviet input for his next book. Politely, I listened to Mr. Bykov tell us about a school in Staten Island, even though I thought it was completely irrelevant.

My mind wandered. Mr. Bykov was an older gentleman. He probably witnessed first-hand the horrors of the siege of Moscow and Leningrad. He probably saw starving Russians eating the bark off trees, and saw countless corpses. For him, I am sure that co-existence is paramount. "Especially in a nuclear age", I heard myself say. I said this without thinking, just being in tune with the situation. Bykov looked stunned.

According to "News for Assemblyman Thomas P. DiNapoli" dated February 7, 1989:

"Assemblyman Thomas P. DiNapoli (D-Great Neck) has announced the delivery to Soviet officials of Assembly Resolution 24, calling upon the government of the Soviet Union to release all prison records regarding Raoul Wallenberg. Working closely with Sharon Wallenberg, President of the Raoul Wallenberg Committee of Long Island, DiNapoli asked that the Soviets invoke the spirit of 'glasnost' and allow the world to confirm the fate of the renowned humanitarian once and for all. Senator Norman Levy (R-Freeport) sponsored the resolution in the Senate.

The resolution was placed on its own special calendar in both the Assembly and Senate, and passed both houses unanimously on January 17. 'January 17 marks the anniversary of the last day of Raoul Wallenberg's freedom and the first day of his captivity,' said Ms. Wallenberg. Raoul Wallenberg, the Swedish native credited with saving the lives of thousands of innocent people during the Second World War, disappeared while in Soviet custody on January 17, 1945.

Assemblyman Alan Hevesi (D-Forest Hills) helped prepare the resolution, which was co-sponsored by seventy Members of Assembly. Long Island Assemblymembers who were co-sponsors included: the Hon. Lewis Yevoli (co-prime sponsor), Daniel Frisa (co-prime sponsor), Gregory Becker, Earlene Hill, George Madison, Charles O'Shea and Frederick Parola of Nassau County, and the Hon. Thomas Barraga, John Cochrane, Robert Gaffney, Paul Harenberg, John Powell and Robert Sweeney of Suffolk County.

A delegation consisting of Assemblyman DiNapoli, Ms. Wallenberg, Rabbi Frederick Werbell, (a noted authority on Wallenberg) and Phyllis Joseph presented the Resolution to the Soviet officials.

Raoul Wallenberg was recruited by the War Refugee Board, established by President Roosevelt during World War II, for a dangerous mission in Nazi-controlled Hungary. Functioning as a Swedish diplomat, Wallenberg worked at great personal peril to provide 'safe conduct passes' to Hungarian Jews targeted for extermination in death camps in Eastern Europe. Because of Wallenberg's work and the work of other humanitarian organizations and individuals, some 120,000 out of the 700,000 Jews in Hungary survived the Nazi plans for genocide. On January 17, 1945 Wallenberg was taken to the Russian front by a two-person escort, ostensibly to discuss arrangement for emergency supplies for the Jewish ghettos in Hungary. He was arrested on charges of spying and was held in Lubianka Prison in Moscow.

The Soviet Union has claimed that Wallenberg died sometime in 1947, but has produced neither his remains nor any other evidence of his death. Throughout the years, there have been a number of reported sightings of Wallenberg, still alive and in Soviet custody.

'The Raoul Wallenberg issue', said DiNapoli, "is certainly not dead. Legislators from around the state have been distributing copies of the resolution to local groups, trying to raise public awareness of the situation."

Mr. DiNapoli and Ms. Wallenberg appealed to the Soviets as Long Island neighbors to make a good faith effort to reveal all the pertinent facts in the case, making reference to the Soviet Mission in Glen Cove."

In addition to presenting the Soviet officials with the New York State Resolution, we also gave them the petition signed by numerous local elected officials at the Demonstration, as well as letters from many other elected officials, demanding the release of Raoul Wallenberg's prison records.

The meeting was the first of its kind between Soviet officials and interested citizens and elected officials to discuss Wallenberg. It lasted for about one hour. Mr. Bykov did not deviate from the official Soviet position that Raoul Wallenberg died in prison in 1947. He did express sympathy and compassion regarding the issue which he referred to as 'sad'. He mentioned the cases of several other Soviet notables whose prison records were lost."

Tom tried his best at the meeting, and I should have been grateful. Instead, all I could think of was that he was too young. He was a young, single man, very charming and supportive, but I thought he was too young. I felt our lack of accomplishing our goal was due to Tom's inexperience. I was wrong, but didn't know it then.

All I could think of was that I needed an older, more experienced person. I needed someone like Bob Mrazek. He was older, more experienced, married, and had two children. He would be perfect. I was convinced this would work if only I had Bob Mrazek instead of Tom DiNapoli with me. "I'm coming back with my Congressman," I said over, and over.

Instead of being turned off, the Soviet officials were delighted. They were delighted to host my Congressman, and expressed their avid desire to meet him. One thing that never occurred to us in this pleasant, cordial environment was that the Soviets did not have Raoul Wallenberg.

As always, I followed up with thank you letters. I thanked Ambassador Belognov for the opportunity to meet with Soviet officials to discuss the release of the prison records of Raoul Wallenberg. To Demitri Bykov, I wrote:

"Thank you very much for your warm and cordial reception at the Soviet Mission. I was really delighted to meet you and Mr. Lukyanovich.

Although I was not able to achieve my goals, I was intrigued with your ideas. You remind me of someone who plants dates even though those who plant them will never eat them. Your deceptively simple idea of Soviet children in U.S. schools may prove to be one of the most effective ways of achieving peace.

The United States is in a period of 'declining enrollment' in schools. With fewer babies being born, the existing educational facilities are becoming more empty. We would welcome the new students for their visit! We have more than enough room! Everyone I have spoken to about this idea is enthusiastic! In order to explore the possibilities of implementing these ideas, I have written to officials on the Municipal, County, State, and Federal levels as well as the Bishop of our Diocese. I will keep you informed of their responses.

Although it has not been since World War II that the U.S. and the Soviet Union were allies, I hope that our two countries can become allies in the endeavor to create Peace in a Nuclear Age.

On a more personal note, I would really enjoy the opportunity to show you the beautiful Russian architecture and icons in Sea Cliff. Perhaps someday when you are in Glen Cove, you will be able to visit me for a few minutes. My apologies that my Russian is so limited. I will add some more words and phrases, but unfortunately will never be fluent.

Please do whatever you can to try to locate some information on Raoul Wallenberg. There is growing interest in this country, and all over the world regarding the fate of this great hero.

I look forward to seeing you again, and salute you as a Peacemaker."

One thing was certain. I had every intention of meeting with the Soviets again, and next time with my Congressman!

Chapter Thirteen:
Time To Shop For A Senator

Naturally, I did get in touch with my Congressman, Bob Mrazek, as soon as possible. I asked him to introduce the DiNapoli Resolution in the U S Congress. He did.

Congressman Robert Mrazek introduced House Concurrent Resolution 165, asking the Soviet Union to release the prison records of Raoul Wallenberg, in the United States House of Representatives on July 12, 1989.

According to the newsletter from Congressman Bob Mrazek, Third District, New York, dated July 12, 1989:

"Resolution Seeks to Answer Mystery of Wallenberg's Fate"

"Washington—U.S. Rep. Robert J. Mrazek (D-Centerport) today introduced a resolution in the House calling on the Soviet Union to 'release the prison records of Raoul Wallenberg and account for his whereabouts.'

The sense-of-the-Congress resolution, cosigned by 72 members, seeks to clear up the mysteries surrounding Wallenberg's fate since he was taken into 'protective custody' by the Soviets in 1945, then arrested on charges of spying. The Soviet Union has maintained that Wallenberg died in prison of a heart attack in 1947 at age 35, but neither his remains nor evidence of his death have been forthcoming.

'Raoul Wallenberg's actions during World War II were indeed a portrait of selfless courage', Rep. Mrazek said. 'His efforts saved the lives of thousands of innocent Jews from the Nazi death machine and remain an inspiration in the cause of human rights today.

Wallenberg, a Swedish diplomat went to Budapest in 1944 at the request of the U.S. War Refugee Board and the World Jewish Congress to organize rescue efforts for Hungarian Jews threatened by Nazi death camps. His efforts resulted in the issuance of protective Swedish passports to more than 15,000 Hungarian Jews, and he is credited with having helped about 100,000 others escape Nazi plans for their extermination.

On January 17, 1945, Wallenberg traveled with Soviet agents to the Russian front, ostensibly to discuss arrangements for emergency supplies to be sent to the Jewish ghettos in Hungary. He was then taken into custody by the Soviets in violation of international standards of diplomatic immunity.

Various accounts over the years have indicated that Wallenberg may still be alive and in Soviet custody.

The resolution specifically calls on the Soviet Union to release Wallenberg's prison records and to account for his whereabouts, and requests President Bush to pursue the matter through diplomatic channels."

Bob circulated a "Dear Colleague" letter asking other Members of Congress to join him in supporting a resolution that may help us understand what has happened to Raoul Wallenberg. The Resolution expresses the sense of Congress "that the Soviet Union should release he prison records of Raoul Wallenberg and account for his whereabouts."

At about the same time, I wrote to Bob telling him that I wrote to President Bush asking for his support on this issue. My letter said in part:

"President Reagan signed an Act of Congress making Raoul Wallenberg an Honorary American Citizen on October 5, 1981. He did this because   Raoul

Wallenberg was one of the greatest heroes that ever lived. Our nation shall always be indebted to Raoul Wallenberg for the miraculous work he did on behalf of President Roosevelt's War Refugee Board.

It is time for you to take action on behalf of Raoul Wallenberg. Please lend your support to a Resolution introduced in Congress by Representative Robert Mrazek to demand the release of the Soviet prison records of Raoul Wallenberg."

In addition, I mentioned to Bob that I received a letter from Congressman Thomas Downey regarding a Soviet / American student exchange program in Sayville, Long Island. I asked if an agency or program could be set up in Washington or New York which could send out a periodic newsletter to all School Districts informing them of existing programs and offering help in creating their own exchange programs. This Peace Initiative seemed like a great idea to build the security of the next generation with friendships started now. I even suggested incorporating this idea into the Resolution.

I also asked if Bob would join me in a meeting with the Soviets in New York. I knew they would love to meet him.

The successful Washington Resolution may have made it feel like it was time for a celebration, but really it wasn't. The House Resolution needed a Companion Resolution in the U.S. Senate. It was time to shop for a Senator.

Chapter Fourteen:
No Senate Sponsor

The first thing I did was to write to all one hundred U.S. Senators. I needed a Senate sponsor to introduce a companion Resolution to the Mrazek Resolution in the House. Ideally, the Senator would be a Republican, since Congressman Bob Mrazek was a Democrat. Bi-partisan support is desirable. Additionally, a Senator from the West Coast would give balanced geographic support.

When I mentioned writing to one hundred Senators at one of the lectures I was giving, a senior woman gasped, "All those stamps!" As it turned out, unasked, a local business woman donated an ample supply of stamps. People were anxious to help in any way they could.

Senator Pete Wilson, a Republican from California, responded telling me he referred my letter to the State Department because that office has jurisdiction over his issue. He offered to be in touch as soon as he received a reply. I already knew of the State Department's level of interest, which was none.

Senator Bill Bradley, a Democrat from New Jersey, also responded to my letter, and enclosed a copy of his letter to Ambassador Dubinin in the Soviet Embassy in Washington, which said in part:

"Since his capture, many attempts have been made to learn the truth about Mr. Wallenberg's fate in the Soviet Union. While the Soviets state that he died of a heart attack in 1947, reports have reached the West that he was seen in the Blagoveshchenka Prison as recently as 1986.

Soviet government officials, including Prime Minister Ryzhov and Ambassador Kashlev have recently acknowledged humanity's debt to this great man.

The relations between our two governments have improved considerably in recent years, in part due to the new era of glasnost. I hope that, in recognition of this spirit, the Soviet government will soon be able to give a definitive report on Mr. Wallenberg, to the family, to those so deeply indebted to him, and to all of us concerned about our relations with our fellow man."

When I thanked Senator Bradley for his interest in Raoul Wallenberg and letter to Ambassador Dubnin, I called it one of the most beautiful letters I had ever read in my life. I went on to say how impressed I was with the work he had done in the Senate regarding the Third World debt problem. I mentioned that I had studied economics on the Doctoral level at Fordham University, and that I had visited the third world as a guest of Food For the Poor, a Catholic Relief Agency. His fair, level-headed and sound approach to this important issue impressed me. It was after reading the Hearing on

International Debt, which Senator Bradley chaired that I had decided he was the right Senator for the Raoul Wallenberg Resolution.

Doing a little further research, I discovered that Senator Bill Bradley was a former ball player. Although I know nothing about sports, I do know that ball players are very popular. My heart was set on Senator Bill Bradley for the Senate Sponsor of the Wallenberg Resolution. Unfortunately, although a very strong supporter, Senator Bradley did not want to take the lead on this. We were left with no Senate sponsor.

One day I was on the phone with Senator Moynihan's office in regard to my upcoming Demonstration for Raoul Wallenberg's birthday in August. The person I was speaking to was a summer intern. Although this is a fabulous experience for a young person, it is the lowest of the low politically. I said to the young man, "There is no Senate sponsor". He replied, "No Senate sponsor?"

I confirmed, "No Senate sponsor". That was all that was said.

The next day nothing happened. Then following day, I received a phone call from Senator Moynihan's office. Senator Daniel Patrick Moynihan introduced Senate Concurrent Resolution 60 seeking the Soviet release of Raoul Wallenberg's prison records in the United States Senate as a companion to the Mrazek Resolution in the House.

Chapter Fifteen:
Hugs and Handshakes

August 4, 1989 was the 77th birthday of Raoul Wallenberg. To commemorate this event, I planned another demonstration across the street from the Soviet residence on Dosoris Lane in Glen Cove.

This time, in addition to asking for Police permission, sending out press releases, invitations, and contacting elected officials and Steve Berman, the free-lance photographer, I also invited the Soviet officials, Ambassador Alexander Belognov, Demetri Bykov, and Vadim Lukyaanovich.

My invitation to Ambassador Belognov stated that elected officials and the general public would attend. An appearance by the Ambassador, or a representative, would be a strong gesture of unified Soviet and American heartbreak over the tragic fate of our beloved hero, Raoul Wallenberg.

Further, I informed him that a Resolution asking for the release of the prison records of Wallenberg would pass in the House and Senate in Washington.

My invitation to Demitri Bykov was friendlier. It said in part, "May I take this opportunity to again thank you for the lovely meeting we had in January. I don't know if I mentioned this before, but your hair, eyes, and manner remind me of my father who died in 1978. So I liked you right away. I also felt a certain closeness when we both thought of how important it is in today's nuclear climate for Soviet and American children to have the opportunity to meet and develop friendships. I have explored the possibilities of furthering existing programs or creating new ones, and it looks promising."

The Soviets accepted. They apologized that Ambassador Belognov could not attend because he would be in Moscow.

By this time, I had become an expert in creating an interesting program, and there was always cake from Hubie. During the event, at one point, I felt my arms floating up, without my participation, and they landed on the Soviet official in a hug. It was not my idea. I can only attribute it to Divine Intervention due to days of fasting.

The Soviet officials were very warm and cordial. They kept asking when the Resolutions in Washington would pass. Actually, we had no idea, but didn't realize it then. The Soviets kept asking Assemblyman Tom DiNapoli, probably thinking he would know since he was a Legislator. Tom kept telling them it would be soon. In reality there is a big difference between Albany and Washington, and how long it takes legislation to pass. The answer we were giving, believing it to be true, was early fall. This probably added fuel to the fire for a quick resolution of the situation

Although we did not realize it then, the Soviets had done their research, and were ready to release the prison records of Raoul Wallenberg. They were apparently playing "beat the clock" with the legislation in Washington.

As usual, I followed up with thank you letters to the Soviet officials, Demitri Bykov, Valentin Lozinskiy, and Vladimir Parsnikov. My letter to Valentin Lozinskiy said in part,

"I was very pleased by your positive remarks and willingness to try to resolve this issue, as well as your personal warmth and sincerity.

There is presently a resolution in the U.S. House of Representatives and Senate to request the release of the prison records of Raoul Wallenberg. It should pass in the early fall. At that time, I would like to have the opportunity to personally present them to you with Congressman Robert Mrazek at your Mission in New York."

To Vladimir Parsnikov I wrote in part,

"Although I did not really have time to get to know you, it certainly put a little excitement in our lives when you had a conversation with my twelve year old daughter, Marisa. I am looking forward to seeing you again."

Although the Soviets did not deviate from the official Soviet statement that Raoul Wallenberg died in prison in 1947, they were very warm and cordial. They made very positive remarks, and were willing to create and maintain a dialogue on the Wallenberg issue. They also expressed sadness about the Soviet citizens also missing in the Gulag.

The following month, the Soviets invited me and Senator Moynihan to visit them in Manhattan. On September 21, 1989, there was a plane crash at LaGuardia. No flights were arriving from Washington. Senator Moynihan was unable to come to New York for the meeting. John Matthews, representing Senator Moynihan, and I went to Manhattan to visit the Soviets.

While we were walking down the street to the mission, John pointed out several cameras which I had been oblivious to. He told me which ones were theirs, and which ones were ours. It really felt like we were living in a cold war.

When we arrived, the guard would not let us in. Vladimir Parshikov came out, and reprimanded the guard in Russian. The guard pointed to John's briefcase, and spoke in Russian. Vladimir apologized to John, and told him that he was not allowed to bring in a briefcase. John said, "It's okay – we do the same thing."

The reason that the Soviets invited us to a meeting at their mission was to ask that the Resolution seeking the release of Raoul Wallenberg's prison records be delayed. The Soviets had invited the Swedish relatives to Moscow to receive the records in

August, but the relatives had delayed their visit until October. Apparently, the Soviets wanted it to look voluntary, not forced. But why did the Swedes delay?

Chapter Sixteen:

Indian Summer

Honorary Citizen Day, October 7, 1989 was celebrated with a concert of inspirational Swedish music after asking permission from Glen Cove Police Chief Timothy Edwards. It was the Eight Anniversary of the Act of Congress which made Raoul Wallenberg one of the few Honorary American Citizens. I borrowed a piano from my friend, Rick Smith, owner of the Piano Exchange in Glen Cove. He had it delivered to, and returned it from, the area in front of the High School, across the street from the Soviet residence on Dororis Lane in Glen Cove. Thanks Rick!

The 'Y', also on Dosoris Lane, was nice enough to lend us chairs for the occasion. Ingrid Olsen, a former Viking Princess, was the singer, and her husband, Richard Feingold, was the pianist. They were neighbors of a relative of mine in Baldwin. It was lovely October weather, and the perfect day for an outdoor event. We were again joined by Soviet officials, Deputy Representative Valentin Lozinskiy, Deputy Representative Demetri Bykov, and Second Secretary Vladimir Parshikov, whom I had invited.

District Attorney Denis Dillon and I invited the Soviet officials to visit Our Lady of Kazan, a Russian church in Sea Cliff. The Nassau County Detectives were present. Usually there are three different kinds of Law Enforcement personnel present when the Soviet officials attended a public function, Glen Cove Police, Nassau County detectives, and the Secret Service. We asked the Soviets to include an American at the meeting in Moscow in order to have a neutral third party present since I expected the possibility of a controversy.

Denis offered to help by playing "Good Cop / Bad Cop." Denis was a policeman before going to Law School at Fordham. Then the family moved to Long Island. Denis served as District Attorney from 1974 through 2005. I appreciated his help and support, but I told him I didn't want to *play* anything.

The Soviets agreed, and said that the request should come from Congressman Mrazek's office. When I asked, Bob agreed.

The Concert was lovely. It was followed by a coffee and Hubie's cake reception at Saint Paul's Church. Steve Berman graciously took photos of the event.

The Soviets were charming as usual. Mr. Bykov even called the gorgeous weather "Indian Summer". He impressed me by knowing an American expression. I knew we were getting closer to learning the true fate of Raoul Wallenberg, and securing his release.

Follow-Up on Wallenberg Vigil

A candle-light vigil was held for Raoul Wallenberg at the Soviet Mission in Glen Cove on Sunday, January 17, 1988. Raoul Wallenberg is the Swedish diplomat and honorary U.S. citizen, who at the request of the U.S. War Refugee Board, went to Budapest during World War II and is credited with saving 100,000 lives. He did this using courage, imagination and determination and at great personal risk.

On January 17, 1945, Mr. Wallenberg was taken into Soviet custody during their liberation of Budapest and never released. Evidence of his imprisonment proliferated followed by mysterious deaths of witnesses. Amnesty International confirms that Raoul Wallenberg is alive in Soviet prison.

The vigil appeared on Long Island Cable TV News 12 and was covered by the local press. Mayor Donald De Riggi of Glen Cove, Councilman Steven Gonzalez, and Robert Zimmerman for Congressman Mrazek were in attendance as well as members of the Jewish Community and Saint Boniface Martyr Church in Sea Cliff.

There will be a follow-up letter writing campaign. All are invited to participate.

Please send politely worded letters requesting information on the whereabouts of Raoul Wallenberg to Secretary General Mikhail Gorbachev, Moscow, USSR and President Ronald Reagan, Washington, D.C.

Additional information is available from: The Raoul Wallenberg Committee of Long Island, Post Office Box 115, Glenwood Landing, N.Y. 11547.

BIRTHDAY FOR RAOUL WALLENBERG was celebrated on Friday evening, in front of the Soviet Mission on Dosoris Lane. Here, Sharon Wallenberg of Sea Cliff, read the history of Wallenberg's assistance to victims of persecution, and his imprisonment by the Soviets, to interested spectators. According to verified reports, Wallenberg is still alive and in prison. Onlookers enjoyed a birthday cake in celebration of Wallenberg's 76 birthday.

Nassau County District Attorney Denis
Dillon, Assemblyman Lewis Yevoli,
Sharon Wallenberg, Rebekah Brown
CountyExecutiveThomas Gulotta,
Assemblyman Thomas DiNapoli.
October 1988

Above: Sharon Wallenberg and then
Assemblyman Thomas P. DiNapoli

Below: Author Rabbi Frederick Werbell

Sharon Wallenberg and

Glen Cove Mayor Donald DiRiggi

Rabbi Frederick Werbell,
Glen Cove City Councilman
Steve Gonzales,
Sharon Wallenberg, and Olivia Lieb
at coffee and cake gathering after
Demonstration

JANUARY 1989

Photo by Steve Berman

Raoul Wallenberg Protest

Demonstrators yesterday outside Soviet compound in Glen Cove sign petition demanding prison records of Raoul Wallenberg, the Swedish diplomat credited with saving thousands of Jews from the Nazis. On the table is a model of a commemorative statue to be erected in Glen Cove. Moscow says he died in a Soviet jail in 1947.

Sharon Wallenberg,
Soviet official Demetri Bykov,
Nassau District Attorney Denis Dillon,
Nassau County Executive Thomas Gulotta,
Assemblyman Thomas Dinapoli.
August 1989.

Soviet Official Valentin Lozinskiy, Ann
Hunt, Sharon Wallenberg, August 1989.

Gulotta Demonstrates on behalf of Raoul Wallenberg, who was a Swedish Diplomat imprisoned by the Soviet Union on Jan. 17, 1945. Since January 1988 the Raoul Wallenberg Committee
of Long Island has been holding demonstrations at the Soviet Union Compound in Glen Cove,
requesting the record of the where-abouts of Raoul Wallenberg. Also participating in the demonstration were: Sharon Wallenberg, who works in Great Neck, committee president; Demetri Bykor,
deputy of legal affairs concerning the U.S.S.R.'s permanent mission to the United States; District
Attorney Denis Dillon; and Thomas DiNapoli.

Newsday August 1989

EDITORIAL

Happy birthday, Raoul Wallenberg

As birthday celebrations go, it was a small gathering — fewer than 20 people — with the traditional chorus of "Happy Birthday" sung soft and low, more somber than jubilant.

The gathering outside the Soviet Mission in Glen Cove last Sunday was attended by County Executive Thomas Gulotta, District Attorney Denis Dillon and several Soviets from the mission, amidst an atmosphere of Glasnost, handshakes and hugs.

But the guest of honor, who would be 77 years old now, was absent. Raoul Wallenberg, a Swedish diplomat, has been missing since January 17, 1945, when he was detained in war-torn Hungary by the Soviets.

The Soviet Union alleges he died in 1947 but some believe there is enough evidence to suggest he may still be alive today in a Soviet prison.

Whether alive or dead, Wallenberg is a living hero. Amidst the horror of World War II, he worked within Nazi-occupied Hungary saving the lives of thousands of Jews by issuing protective passes, setting up safe houses and rescuing those he could from the death marches and deportation trains.

For years the Soviets have been asked to supply concrete information on the fate of Raoul Wallenberg, such as his prison records, to prove that he did indeed die in 1947 as they allege. No information has been forthcoming.

Now, in the midst of Glasnost, The Raoul Wallenberg Committee of Long Island (P.O. Box 45, Sea Cliff, N.Y. 11579) is trying once again.

Last Sunday, petitions were distributed among those who attended — petitions requesting that the Soviets finally release Wallenberg's prison records, and let the world know the fate of this "living hero."

Let's hope the hugs and handshakes that highlighted the celebration of Wallenberg's 77th birthday by Soviets and Americans are truly a sign of new efforts on both sides to determine the fate of this "living hero" once and for all.

138

Indian Summer Concert. Flora Musico,
Soviet Official Demetri   Bykov. October
1989.

A Special Vigil for a Special Hero

By Carol Eisenberg

Three times a year, every year, in good weather and bad, Sharon Wallenberg of Sea Cliff has stood in front of the Soviet mission in Glen Cove demanding the prison records of Raoul Wallenberg, saviour of thousands of Hungarian Jews.

Yesterday, on the eve of the holy Jewish day of remembrance and atonement, Yom Kippur, Wallenberg organized what she hopes will be the final gathering on behalf of the Swedish diplomat who saved tens of thousands of Jews from Nazi death camps and then disappeared into a Soviet prison camp, never to be heard from again.

"This is possibly the last demonstration because the Soviets seem to be cooperating at last — they have invited the brother and sister of Raoul Wallenberg, as well as a Swedish ambassador, to a meeting in Moscow next week," said Wallenberg, who is no relation to the diplomat but who has devoted eight years to finding out about him. Officials at the Soviet mission confirmed the visit.

The haunting story of Raoul Wallenberg dates to the last days of World War II, when the U.S. government asked neutral Sweden to try to protect Hungarian Jews from extermination. The Swedes agreed to send a young diplomat to Budapest, where Nazi leader Adolf Eichmann was supervising the deportation of Jews.

Almost overnight, Raoul Wallenberg — the scion of a distinguished Swedish family — became a mythic figure, confounding all expectations of what one man could do against Nazi terror. Using Swedish neutrality, diplomatic status and some funds from American Jews, he distributed thousands of protective Swedish passports, housed Jews in safe houses draped with Swedish flags and is said to have snatched people right off the death lines.

In January, 1945, Wallenberg went to meet the victorious Soviet army in Budapest to seek help and promptly disappeared. Initially, the Soviets denied he had been there. But in 1957, faced with growing world demands about his disappearance, the Kremlin acknowledged that Wallenberg had died in a Soviet prison in 1947.

Still, sightings of him were reported regularly. In the late 1970s, a Soviet dissident reported after his release that he had met a Swedish prisoner held in jail for more than 30 years.

Sharon Wallenberg, who said she has been following the Swedish hero's case since reading a newspaper article about him in 1980, doesn't presume to know whether he's alive or dead. But she said she will not rest until she finds out.

"I wasn't even born during World War II," said Wallenberg who is Catholic, "but I was touched by his imagination, his compassion and his courage."

She has approached the Soviet mission three times a year on the anniversaries of three significant dates in the case — in January, when Wallenberg disappeared; on his birthday in August; and in October to mark the day he was made an honorary American citizen.

Yesterday's gathering was timed to coincide with the date Wallenberg received honorary American citizenship, rather than with the Jewish high holiday. But a member of the American Jewish Congress said that recalling Wallenberg's courageous fight is particularly apt on the eve of Yom Kippur.

"Yom Kippur is a time for remembrance and introspection and this is also the 50th anniversary of the start of World War II," said Carol Siegel of Glen Cove, president of the Long Island Young Professional's chapter of the American Jewish Congress. "I think this is a very appropriate time to think of this man who saved so many Jewish lives and how he may still be alive in the Soviet gulag."

Chapter Seventeen:
Soviets Release
Wallenberg's Prison Records

In August 1989, the then Soviet Union invited Raoul Wallenberg's half-sister, Nina Lagergren, and half-brother, Guy Von Dardle, to Moscow to receive Raoul Wallenberg's prison records and his remaining personal items. They did not go.

Instead, while maintaining that Wallenberg was languishing away in prison, suffering every minute, they went to Washington D.C. Why? They met with Congressman Tom Lantos who had nothing to do with the release of Raoul Wallenberg's prison records. While in Washington, they were honored at a special black tie dinner.

When they finally went to Moscow in October, they were treated with the utmost courtesy and respect. They were given records and personal items. Prisons were opened up to them. The list of witnesses and claims that they brought with them were looked into. Soviet TV asked the Soviet public for help in finding Raoul Wallenberg.

No evidence emerged to support the claim that Raoul Wallenberg was alive. At the end, the Swedes presented the Soviets with their hotel bill.

Soviet Official Second Secretary Vladimir Parshikov mailed me a copy of an article "Is The Case of Raoul Wallenberg Closed?" published in the December issue of a Soviet magazine "Mezhdunarodnaya Zhizn" ("International Life") which said:

"The name of Raoul Wallenberg, who went missing at the very end of World War II, did not become widely known in our country until recently. Not everything is clear to this day either about the arrest in 1945 of the Swedish diplomat, who heroically saved thousands of people from death in Nazi prisons in Hungary, or about his last days.

In October 1989, Raoul Wallenberg's stepsister Nina Lagergren and stepbrother Guy von Dardle visited Moscow together with Per Anger, Chairman of the Raoul Wallenberg Association, and Sonia Sonnenfeldt, its Secretary.

Following are the texts of records of the conversations which the Swedish visitors had at the Soviet Foreign Ministry.

Conversation between Valentin Nikiforov, Deputy Minister for Foreign Affairs of the USSR, Vladimir Pirozhkov, Deputy Chairman of the USSR State Security Committee, Raoul Wallenberg's relatives and the leadership of the Raoul Wallenberg Association.

October 16, 1999. On instructions from the leadership of the USSR Ministry of Foreign Affairs and the USSR State Security Committee, V. Nikiforov and V. Pirozhkov received Raoul Wallenberg's stepsister Nina Lagergren and stepbrother Guy Von Dardle as well as the Chairman of the Raoul Wallenberg Association, Per Anger, and its Secretary, Sonja Sonnenfeldt.

During the conversation that took place, the Soviet participants emphasized that the Soviet leadership and Soviet people extended their deepest sympathy to Raoul Wallenberg's relatives over the tragic fate which that outstanding Swedish diplomat had met. The exploit accomplished by him to save people in the war years was admired in the Soviet Union. His noble activity had won universal recognition and respect in our country.

The invitation for the Swedish representatives to arrive in Moscow for a conversation had been prompted by the need to set out the Soviet view of Wallenberg's fate and to put at the visitors' disposal evidence likely to arouse their interest.

As for what happened to the Swedish diplomat, it was stated in the most explicit terms that, regrettably, the Soviet side could tell nothing new concerning the circumstances of Wallenberg's arrest or the reason for it. A cruel war had been on at the time, with millions losing their lives in its maelstrom or disappearing without leaving a trace. However, it had been established as far back as 1957 that Raoul Wallenberg, like many thousands of both Soviet and foreign citizens, had fallen victim to the illegal practices rife in the years of Stalinist rule.

Repeated attempts to ascertain the reason for Wallenberg's imprisonment had unfortunately produced no results. The Soviet side believes the relevant documents and other records were destroyed by the agency controlled by Beria, Abakumov and others of that ilk. It was common knowledge that these men had been punished according to their deserts by being shot for their crimes. The only evidence of

Raoul Wallenberg's death that had been discovered was a report by Dr. A. Smoltsov, chief of the medical services in Lubyanka prison; the report said that the Swedish diplomat had died on July 17, 1947, presumably of a heart attack.

On September 22, 1989 officers of the USSR State Security Committee discovered in the Committee's archives some documents and personal effects that are believed to belong to Raoul Wallenberg.

Thus the earlier explanation offered to the Swedish side on various levels and in various periods after February 1957 stood, nor could the Soviet side add anything to it with the best will in the world.

Much as everyone lamented it, Raoul Wallenberg was no more; he had died long ago, and this must be reckoned with for all that it was distressing. His memory, the memory of his noble work, would always remain in the hearts and minds of all progressive people.

The Swedes were handed a copy (and shown the original) of Dr. Smoltsov's report; a copy of the registration card made out in prisoner Raoul Wallenberg's name in the Inner Prison of the USSR People's Commissariat of State Security on February 6, 1945; two identity cards – Nos. 1369 and 06464 – in his name; and money (US Dollars, Swiss francs, Swedish kronor, Hungarian pengos, Bulgarian leva, Reichs mark) and objects believed to have belonged to him (two food rations cards, two notebooks, a powder-case).

The Swedish interlocutors said that they appreciated the invitation to come to Moscow for a meeting with representatives of the Soviet Foreign Ministry and the State Security Committee.

While noting that they saw as an obvious change in the attitude of the Soviet authorities and Soviet public opinion to the inquiry into the 'Wallenberg case', they affirmed, nevertheless, that neither the explanation offered them nor the documents and personal belongings turned over to them were any proof at all that Wallenberg had died in 1947. After accepting very coolly and rather distrustfully the documents and objects handed over, they began citing 'witnesses' testimony, saying that it indirectly 'confirmed' the case that the Soviet authorities had still kept Wallenberg in various prisons in the fifties, seventies and even 'about 1980'.

'To make their point, they presented a list of 'witnesses', with a brief exposition of their testimony to the effect that Wallenberg was living after 1947. Thereupon they asked for comment.

'The Soviet side told them that it was very difficult if possible at all to check the testimony on its merits, since some of the witnesses on the list were dead. Still, an effort would be made to check what could be checked, and the Swedish representatives would be answered accordingly.

In conclusion the Swedes pointed out that the conversation had proceeded in a "most friendly atmosphere".

October 20, 1989 As agreed, V. Nikiforov and V. Pirozhkov received Raoul Wallenberg's relatives and the representatives of the Raoul Wallenberg Association for a final conversation.

V. Nikiforov noted that the Soviet side, which strove to help as best it could in ascertaining Raoul Wallenberg's fate and proceeded in compliance with the wishes of his relatives and the Association's leadership, had for several days after the first conversation studied some of the testimony cited by the Swedes. It had checked the list of 'witnesses' handed to the Soviet representatives on October 16, 1989. The work done had led to the conclusion that the dates presented by the Swedish side were indirect and could not serve as proof of the claim that Wallenberg had been kept in Soviet prisons after 1947.

The testimony of Claudio de Mohr, Menachem Melzer, Emil Erugger and those others who were no more should be dismissed out of hand, for it was impossible to verify the facts given by them.

There was every reason to describe as untenable the assertion made by Professor Nonna Svartz of Sweden, who claimed with reference to a conversation with Alexander Myasnikov, a Soviet scientist, that Raoul Wallenberg had been confined in a mental clinic. Her claim was disapproved by a record of the conversations which Myasnikov had had with her on July 6, 1965, and with the then Ambassador of Sweden to the USSR, Gunnar Jarring, on May 11, 1965. Present here was Ambassador Extraordinary and Plenipotentiary Georgi Farafonov (ret.), who had served as a counselor in the Soviet Foreign Ministry's Department of Scandinavian Countries. He had recorded Myasnikov's conversation with Svartz and could give exhaustive answers to questions about the Soviet scientist's 'utterances'. We handed copies of those conversations to the Swedish side.

V. Pirozhkov dwelt at length on the results of three days of work done by State Security officers to check the testimony set out in the Swedish list. He stressed that the officers, realizing the need for an objective and the fullest possible restoration of all the facts relating to Wallenberg's fate, had talked to some of the Soviet citizens mentioned in the list.

They had talked to among others, Y. Butova, a surgeon in Vladimir prison from 1946 to 1978. In an explanatory note a copy of which could be made available to the Swedish side, Butova states that she had first heard of Raoul Wallenberg in 1988, from

Soviet Ambassador in Luxemborg A. Avdeyev, who had made inquiries about Wallenberg's fate. Never throughout her surgical practice had she come across any name resembling Wallenberg's.

The officers had also talked to L. Sukhacheva, a doctor in Vladimir prison from 1953 to 1983. She said that never since she took the job had any prisoner by the name of Wallenberg consulted her.

The list mentioned some other staff members of Vladimir prison. It had been established that Captain Nikolayev had served at that prison since 1959, was the deputy chief of that prison, had been pensioned off on account of ill health in 1973 with the rank of lieutenant-colonel and had died in 1988. As for Gulyayev, he had served on the prison staff in the 1953-1962 period with the rank of sergeant. In 1962, he had left Vladimir, and his place of residence at the moment had not yet been established.

With reference to Ann Bilber's testimony about her father Jan Kaplan having seen Wallenberg in Butyrki prison in 1975, we gave the Swedish side copies of explanatory notes written by Kaplan (convicted twice for speculation and once for currency black-marketing) and his wife Budovskaya in 1979 and saying that Kaplan had never met or heard of any prisoner of the name Raoul Wallenberg.

It followed that the check-up had confirmed the absence of any information indicating that Wallenberg was living after 1947.

V. Nikiforov mentioned that East-West talks on exchanging Colonel Stig Wennerstrom which the list said were held from 1965 to 1971. He noted that the Swedish exposition of the basis for the talks and the claim that the two sides had discussed the possibility of exchanging Wennerstrom for Wallenberg were very vague and unclear and that the Swedish side must further specify what evidence in the letter was to be checked.

In the light of the foregoing, any unbiased person would come to the conclusion that the Soviet Union sincerely wanted to help Wallenberg's relatives ascertain the circumstances surrounding his fate. The Soviet side had invited its Swedish interlocutors to Moscow to this end, turned over the Swedish diplomat's papers and personal belongings to them and promptly checked the list of 'witnesses' presented by the Swedes during the first conversation, on October 16, 1989. The guests' claim that Wallenberg was living and was kept in a Soviet prison under a false name could not be confirmed, as the documents made available by the Soviet side indicated.

Hence the Soviet side could not agree with what Nina Lagergren had said in the Soviet Vremya programme telecast on October 19, 1989. From what she had affirmed, the combined testimony of various 'witnesses' invited the conclusion that Wallenberg was living. Yet not a single 'witness's' testimony had passed the test of an impartial check-up. The Soviet side called on Sweden to believe in the sincerity of its efforts towards establishing the truth about Wallenberg's fate. It was ready to go on studying most carefully witnesses' testimony and other evidence should the Swedish side ask for their examination.

The Swedish interlocutors expressed gratitude for the information on the results of the verification of the list. They said they were impressed with the openness and sincerity which the Soviet side had shown during the conversations, seen by them as the beginning of a dialogue aimed at ascertaining Wallenberg's fate.

They pointed out that they did not want to be accused of bias but could not accept the Soviet account of the Swedish diplomat's fate, for they considered that neither Smoltsov's report nor Wallenberg's papers and personal belongings constituted legally authentic proof of his death on July 17, 1947. They would like to check the "Vladimir prison version" by themselves, acquaint themselves with the prisoners' registration card index and question witnesses in Vladimir. With this aim in view, Guy Von Dardle and Sonja Sonnenfeldt were ready to stay in the Soviet Union for a few more days.

V. Nikoforov said that the Soviet side supported the proposal and was willing to help make the trip.

In conclusion, the Swedes again expressed gratitude for the invitation to come for talks to Moscow, the attention they were given, in particular by the Soviet media, and the atmosphere of mutual respect, benevolence and sincerity. Putting it on record that the two sides still differed, they said they would continue their inquiry into the case.

Conversation between Yevgeni Rymko, Deputy Chief, Second European Department of the USSR Ministry of Foreign Affairs, Guy Von Dardle and Sonja Sonnenfeld

October 25, 1989 Y. Rymko received Raoul Wallenberg's stepbrother Guy Von Dardle and the Secretary of the Raoul Wallenberg Association, Sonja Sonnenfeldt, at their request.

The Swedes told him about their visit to Vladimir prison on October 23, 1989 stressing that they had been received very well by the chief of that institution, V. Gorshkov, and his colleagues. Making the reservation that they had not aimed to achieve any big results during so brief a stay in Vladimir, they voiced satisfaction at having been enabled to photograph the registration cards of some of the 'witnesses' in the 'Wallenberg case' who had served time in that prison.

However, they had found the registration cards of some prisoners mentioned in the Swedish side's list of 'witnesses' missing from the prison's card index. Besides, they had encountered difficulties in trying to ascertain the names of the 'witnesses' cellmates, for the cells had been renumbered more than once over the past years.

The Swedes said that they had asked the authorities of Vladimir prison to make inquiries about former Swedish inmates bearing the name of Wallenberg or similar names, such as, say, Fallenberg or Vandenberg, and had been promised help.

In this connection, Von Dardle said that he would like to go to Vladimir for roughly a week to continue studying the prison card index and that he planned to do so together with Professor Marvin Makinen, a Chicago resident who had been imprisoned in Vladimir, as far as the Swedes knew. What they wanted to see primarily was a list of the registration cards as well as, if possible, the files on the persons whom they needed and who had served time in that institution.

Commenting on the copy of the report submitted by Smoltsov, the former chief of the medical service in Lubyanka prison, the Swedish interlocutors called into question the circumstance that both signatures on the document belonged to one and the same person (Smoltsov), and said that, generally speaking, the report was no proof of Wallenberg's death. They added that they would like to acquaint themselves if they might with other documents kept in the same file as Smoltsov's report.

The Soviet Representative expressed his opinion of the assertions questioning the authenticity of Smoltsov's report.

In conformity with the instructions given him, he passed to the Swedes copies of the documents concerning the 'Wallenberg case'.

The Swedes thanked their Soviet interlocutor and said they hoped the search for new documents would be continued, possibly by a joint West-Soviet group which could comprise, apart from Guy Von Dardle and Sonja Sonnenfeldt, Cronid Lubarski (publisher, Munich, FRG), Yuri Louri (professor of law, Ontario, Canada), and Marvin Makinen (professor of biochemistry, Chicago, USA) on the Western side and Academician Andrei Sakharov along with others on the Soviet side.

In reply to Von Dardle's proposal for forming a joint working group that would concern itself with the 'Wallenberg case', the Soviet representative said that, as the Soviet side had stated earlier, it would carefully study new relevant evidence which the Swedes might supply.

In conclusion, the Swedes brought up the issues of the expenses of their stay in the Soviet Union and showed a hotel bill for 37,000 kronor. Saying that they did not consider the matter decisive for them, they asked whether the problem could be settled in a way more favorable to them when they came to Moscow again.

The Soviet representative answered that the Swedish group had been staying in Moscow as guests of the Swedish Ambassador."

Further, according to a Newsday article dated October 6, 1989, "Soviet television asked viewers yesterday night to provide any information they have on Raoul Wallenberg, a Swedish diplomat who saved 100,000 Hungarian Jews from the Nazis, and is said to have died in a Soviet prison camp....Despite Soviet insistence that he died in prison, reports persist that Wallenberg has been seen in Soviet jails."

Back in Long Island, where the pressure to create this investigation started, Assemblyman Tom DiNapoli asked me if the Swedes thanked me for all I had done for Raoul Wallenberg.

"No", I answered. "That's not why I did it".

"I know", Tom replied.

Chapter Eighteen: Amend The Legislation

After the release of Raoul Wallenberg's prison records, and the totally unsubstantiated Swedish claims, I was ambivalent. Determined to find out the truth, I went to visit the Soviets in Manhattan. This was the first time I went alone. Yes, it was a little frightening to go alone, but I had to know the truth.

When I arrived Demitri Bykov and Vladimir Parshikov were still at the United Nations. I was taken to a conference room to wait. It felt like I was there a very long time. My mind wandered to stories of the KGB, and the gulag archipelago. I couldn't remember if I told anyone where I was going. What if I never returned!

Eventually, my Soviet friends, Demetri and Vladimir, arrived full of apologies about the delay at the UN. I was just glad to see them, and know that I would be going home that evening!

We discussed the prison record release. I still expected that there was some catch, something… By this time, I had come to know these men. After listening to Demetri Bykov, I had no doubt in my mind that Raoul Wallenberg was **not** alive in Soviet prison. I just knew.

All I could think of was the work going on in Washington for my resolutions. I expressed concern about it. Vladimir, who was the younger of the two, said "Just let them do it".

"I can't do that!" I responded. Taxpayer dollars pay the salaries of the Legislators and their staff. If this issue is moot, they should be working on some other more relevant issues.

Demitri Bykov had an idea. He suggested amending the legislation to create a joint US – USSR Peace initiative. This made sense.

It would make something positive and meaningful come out of Raoul Wallenberg's selfless sacrifice.

At first this seemed like a very good idea. Unfortunately, not everyone had the opportunity to speak to the Soviets in person. Many people still believed Raoul Wallenberg was alive. I wanted to end this disinformation once, and for all. The sensationalism that surrounded Wallenberg was similar to the then constant rumors that Elvis Presley was still alive. Wallenberg didn't deserve that.

As a longtime member of Amnesty International, I had repeatedly written letters on behalf of people who had disappeared, or been the victims of extra judicial executions. We always asked for an impartial investigation. That seemed like a better idea. This would end the sensationalism, and stop the blaming of the Soviets, which was only causing animosity.

Raoul Wallenberg should be remembered for the good he did, and not be used as a weapon to cause hatred. I attempted to amend the legislation by contacting Congressman Mrazek and Senator Moynihan with the following letter:

"In view of the recent Soviet initiative in Moscow to resolve the disappearance of Raoul Wallenberg, I would like to suggest the following additions to the Resolution:

1) The United States government gratefully acknowledges the presentation of the existing Soviet prison records and personal effects of Raoul Wallenberg to his family. It is further urged that all allegations of sightings of Mr. Wallenberg since July 17, 1945 be thoroughly and impartially investigated and those results made public.

2) At the suggestion of the Soviet government, a joint US-USSR peace initiative should be established in Raoul Wallenberg's honor. Mr. Wallenberg leaves

us a rich legacy, one that is treasured by many nations and every effort should be made to continue it. This initiative should be geared to the future and benefit the most vulnerable members of the world's population, specifically, at this time, the developing nations.

If I can be of any further help with the Resolution, please contact me immediately. Thank you very much for all your efforts on behalf of Raoul Wallenberg.

Sincerely, Sharon Wallenberg"

This simple request for an impartial investigation was met with fierce resistance from an unexpected, behind the scenes advisory.

Chapter Nineteen:
Benign Neglect

After the Swedish relatives were invited to Moscow in August 1989, they went to Washington D.C. to see Congressman Tom Lantos in October 1989. They also met with Congressman Mrazek, as confirmed to me by his aide Kenneth Schwitz on August 22, 1990. Nina Lagergren and Guy Von Dardle asked Congressman Robert Mrazek, my Congressman, to stop working on the Resolution. I suspect that they told Senator Moynihan the same thing. Neither one of my federal elected officials did any work on my Resolution, or communicated with me after that.

Congressman Tom Lantos sent out a Newsletter in December 1989 which grossly misrepresented the nature and purpose of my Resolution. It was basically lies. It was so upsetting to me, that I drove to Washington to see Senator Claiborne Pell, a Democrat from Rhode Island, and Chairman of the Senate Foreign Relations Committee.

When legislation is introduced, it goes into one or more Committees. It must first be voted on in these Committees before going to the full legislature for a vote. After it passes both Houses, it is signed by the Governor or President and becomes law. The Raoul Wallenberg Resolution, introduced at my request, was in the Senate Foreign Relations Committee, which was chaired by Senator Pell.

I drove from Long Island to Washington D.C. in an old, and possibly unreliable, car with my hair in curlers, and wearing comfortable clothes. When I arrived in Washington, I parked as close as I could to the Capitol, and changed my clothes in the car. I could do that - I used to be a model. I styled my hair, and applied make-up, all in the car. Then I raced up the steps of the

Capitol, and found the room where I was meeting Senator Pell.

Senator Pell was a very lovely, peaceful, serene man. One of his aides attended the meeting with us. I listened respectfully to Senator Pell speaking. Then I used the secret weapon. I prayed. At that time I was using a lot of centering prayer, which is the Christian name for meditation. I briefly meditated to open a channel for God's intervention.

The staffer was watching me intently, but said nothing. Senator Pell missed it. Finally in referring to Raoul Wallenberg, Senator Pell said "benign neglect". Without thinking, planning, or even being aware of it, I said loudly, "But Senator Pell, you can't do that!"

I shocked myself. I would never be disrespectful to anyone. I felt ashamed and embarrassed – but it worked. After the meeting with Senator Pell, I received a letter from him dated December 5, 1989, then from Senator Moynihan dated December 11, 1989, and then from Congressman Mrazek dated December 19, 1989. Those three letters are included in the appendix of this book. Everything was back on track. Thank you, God and Senator Pell!

Chapter Twenty:
What's Going On?

The Soviets released the prison records and personal items from Raoul Wallenberg to the Swedish relatives. Nina Lagergren and Guy Von Dardle were still were not satisfied. Every witness and claim the Swedes had brought with them was thoroughly investigated. Prisons were opened to them. Still the Swedish relatives continued to say that Wallenberg was alive.

Why did the Swedes delay going to Moscow for months while still asserting that Raoul Wallenberg was suffering in prison? When in Washington, why did Congressman Tom Lantos direct the Swedes to Congressman Bob Mrazek, and presumably Senator Moynihan, to ask them to stop the Legislation that was responsible for the Soviet openness? Why did they ask Congressman Mrazek to change his mind, and not request that an American to be present for the prison release in Moscow, as he had already agreed?

When the Swedes finally went to Moscow, and had the opportunity to conduct an investigation, what did their investigation show? According to Frederick Werbell, no signature from Wallenberg showed up. This is one way to know if someone is alive. Nana Schwartz, one of the Swede's "witnesses", was interviewed by Werbell. She denied on tape the incident the Swedes were basing their claims on. The investigation in Moscow found no evidence to support the claim that Raoul Wallenberg was alive in a 1,200 page report. Could the Swedish relatives, and Swedish Government be lying?

Betty Throne-Holst, an American, was a neighbor and good friend of Nina Lagergren in Stockholm for fifteen years. Mrs. Throne-Holst never once heard Mrs. Lagergren mention Raoul Wallenberg according to taped interviews with Rabbi Werbell.

Norma Anderson founded a Raoul Wallenberg Committee in Jamestown, New York. Norma wanted to hold a conference to find out the fate of Raoul Wallenberg. She invited all Raoul Wallenberg Committees, and interested people. According to Norma, The Raoul Wallenberg Committee of the United States in Manhattan, which is a direct branch of the Stockholm Wallenberg Committee, discouraged her from doing it. They did not want the focus on discovering the true fate of Raoul Wallenberg, they wanted the goal of the conference to 'inform and inspire'.

Norma told me that on August 3, 1988, Sonya Sonnenfeld, the Executive Secretary of the Stockholm Wallenberg Committee, phoned her and demanded that she not hold the conference to try to discover the true fate of Raoul Wallenberg. Sonnenfeld said the conference would be injurious to the cause of finding out the true fate of Wallenberg, but did not say why. Ultimately, Norma felt pressured into cancelling the conference.

After my first meeting with Assemblyman Thomas DiNapoli and the Soviets on January 26, 1989, Guy Von Dardle called me and thoroughly questioned me. I asked him one question. How did he know that Raoul Wallenberg was alive? Based on what I could hear in his voice, I never said Raoul Wallenberg was alive again in public. He sounded like he was lying through his teeth.

What about Congressman Tom Lantos? According to the Editors at the San Jose Mercury,

"After wading through the slime, it's apparent to us that Lantos has operated as a wheeler-dealer who has been willing to play fast and loose with the rules of propriety". Further they cited Lantos' checkered employment history, which raised doubts about his judgment and financial responsibility.

According to Jewish World, while an elected official, Tom Lantos shipped his Mercedes–Benz around Europe at tax payer expense, as well as giving free charter flights, and other gifts to foreign officials. In addition, Lantos was forced out of the California Teachers Association. When he was Controller and Business Director, he allegedly he gave them poor financial advice causing the CTA to incur a two million dollar deficit.

Tom Lantos became a Congressman in the 1980 election. Lantos was born in Hungary, and survived World War II there. According to Lantos, his wife, Annette, and he were rescued by Wallenberg. The less dramatic reality is that someone in Annette's family was rescued by Wallenberg. I was told he recruited Wallenberg's relatives to create awareness of Raoul Wallenberg. This also created awareness of him. Lantos introduced Legislation in Washington which made

Raoul Wallenberg an Honorary American Citizen. He did nothing to rescue Wallenberg while continuing to maintain that he was alive in Soviet prison.

At one point during the early 1980's, I drove to Washington to meet with Congressman Lantos. I brought my two daughters. I was anxious to see if there was anything I could do to help Raoul Wallenberg. Annette Lantos came out to the waiting area, and asked if I was writing a paper on Wallenberg. I was dismissed without seeing Lantos or even being allowed in the office. The aides looked completely embarrassed at the shabby treatment I was given. I made the trip into a fun outing for my girls, and then went back to Long Island.

As a result of all the talks I was giving on Long Island during the late 80's and early 90's, people always asked me how I was related to Raoul Wallenberg. In order to satisfy the curiosity of these strangers, I asked Nina Lagergren, when she was in

Manhattan, to help me find out. She mailed me something saying that I was not related. I accepted that.

However, one of my friends from Great Neck wanted to see what she had sent me. He told me she did it wrong. That never occurred to me. Then my friend, Joe Wirth, went into Manhattan to the Swedish Consulate. He found a Stockholm phone book, and looked in the yellow pages for a detective.

I contacted the detective in Stockholm, and hired him. I sent $100 bills in the mail. First he traced my Swedish Grandfather forward, and found relatives I did not know I had in Stockholm. I later visited them. Then he traced my Grandfather back to a small village in northern Sweden. It is the same village where Raoul Wallenberg's relatives originally came from. At that point the records were not good. The detective didn't want me to spend any more money for possibly inconclusive results. The results of the search, although inconclusive, created the very strong possibility of a familial connection to Raoul Wallenberg. Ms. Lagergren had totally dismissed that possibility. Was this done on purpose?

I thought the Soviets were the bad guys, and the Swedes were the good guys. What's going on?

Chapter Twenty One
From Demonstrations To Events

Once the Soviets released the prison records and personal effects of Raoul Wallenberg, it did not make sense to hold any more demonstrations. As long as the Swedes continued to maintain that Raoul Wallenberg was alive, there was no closure.

Legislative resolutions in Washington were being amended to seek an impartial investigation. If nothing showed up from the investigation, then Wallenberg could finally rest in peace, and the sensationalism would dissipate. Unfortunately even with Senator Pell's help, the progress was slow at best.

In order to keep the momentum going, I turned to my statue idea, and started holding events rather than demonstrations. Bob

Bernhard, of my Amnesty International Group 17, lived in Sands Point, an upscale area on the North Shore of Long Island. Bob asked his Sands Point friends, Norman and Evelyn Blankman, to donate the use of their Sands Point home. It had an auditorium!

On January 27, 1990, to commemorate Raoul Wallenberg's January 1945 disappearance, I held a flute concert featuring Helene Derwinger. Ms. Deringer is an accomplished Swedish flutist who had played for the Wallenberg family and other members of Swedish society. Helene has Fine Arts degrees from the Royal College of Music in Stockholm and the World Academy of Music, and was then attending Julliard School of Music. I invited the Soviets officials, elected officials, members of the Jewish and Christian Communities where I had given presentations on Raoul Wallenberg, anyone who had participated in previous events, friends, family, and the general public, through press releases.

The Soviet officials, Demetri Bykov and Valentin Lozinsky came, and brought a generous donation for the Wallenberg statue from the Soviet Union. Assemblyman Tom DiNapoli, author Frederick Werbell, the local press, and many supporters were there. It was really lovely!

In my thank you letter to Mr. Bykov and Mr. Lozinskiy I said in part, "I think it is especially important that the Soviet government is involved with us in creating a tribute to this great hero. His courageous acts will thus become a further bridge to a true and lasting peace."

In my thank you letter to Assemblyman Tom DiNapoli I said in part,

"Over the years things have been done to prevent the resolution of this mystery, and in fact, to continue it in a sensational manner. The necessary healing of this tragedy is therefore prevented from taking place. This benefits neither Raoul Wallenberg nor the international community, or allows something positive to be created in his memory.

Please find it in your heart to contribute your thoughts, ideas, values and dedication to resolving this issue. I do not need legislation, I need your input and ideas. This situation has lasted for 40 years, please help end it in a proper manner."

Tom did have an idea. In the meantime, I was still trying to amend the Washington Resolution to seek an impartial investigation in the Soviet Union in the hope that this would end the sensationalism that Raoul Wallenberg was alive in Soviet prison.

Since it was very slow going in Washington, I asked Tom to introduce Legislation in Albany to seek an impartial investigation. And I went forward with exploring his new idea.

Chapter Twenty-Two: The Statue - A Means To An End

The idea of a statue of Raoul Wallenberg was conceived after the Soviets released the prison records of Raoul Wallenberg. At that point, it no longer made sense to hold demonstrations outside the Soviet residence in Glen Cove, since they were co-operating. However, rumors still persisted that Wallenberg was alive in a Soviet prison. The statue was a very good reason to continue to meet, and dialogue.

This was my first time building a statue of Raoul Wallenberg, or anyone else, in Long Island, or anywhere. As a novice, I had to begin somewhere. I started with a local sculptor in Roslyn, and personal friend, George Gach. Gach was born in Hungary, the son of the eminent sculptor, Stephen Gach. George was a graduate of the

Academy of Fine Arts in Budapest. He was a classical multimedia sculptor in wood, stone, bronze, terracotta, plastic, and steel and an impressionist painter. Also, he had been a Professor of Sculpture at the Academy of Fine Arts in Beruit, Lebanon 1947 – 1952. He traveled and worked extensively throughout Europe, the Middle East, North and South America, Mexico and the South Pacific. He had lived on Long Island since 1952.

George made a model of the Wallenberg statue in Budapest to use as an example of what we could do to show at gatherings. He was not sure if he could actually do it, and later suffered an unfortunate accident which prevented him from having the use of his hand.

E. Gyuri Hollosy was the next and final candidate for the Wallenberg statue. I saw a fabulous statue in Boston when visiting my daughter, Becky, at Boston University. I called the city and found out the sculptor was Hollosy. We met in at his home and studio in New Jersey. He and his wife, Marge also came to Long Island to look at the site. They were really lovely people.

E. Gyuri Hollosy was born in Germany to Hungarian parents. He has a Bachelor of Fine Arts from Ohio University, and a Master of Fine Arts from Tulane University. He has teaching experience and many, many commissions, exhibitions, public collections, and has given many lectures and workshops, has published books and films, is affiliated with many galleries, and has many professional memberships. His idea for the Wallenberg statue was brilliant, and I was happy to be working with him.

Nassau County would have been the recipient of the statue. The County would have the responsibility to care for it just like the many estates that are donated to the County to be Museums, or whatever, when their owners can no longer afford the real estate taxes on them. The County was very cooperative and helpful by helping me find a site. I decided on The Cradle of Aviation in Mitchel Field where the first transatlantic flight took place. It seemed like a good choice. I told Guri it had a lot of sky. He told me he liked sky.

I was finding support in the fundraising efforts from names on sign-up sheets from presentations I had given in various places on Long Island. Some of the names had been in the press, and I contacted them to set up meetings. This was a first for me, but I was a quick study.

The statue was a means to an end. Not everyone understood this. Town Supervisor Angelo Delgatti did. This is from my letter to him dated June 2, 1990,

"I wanted to take a moment to let you know how nice it was to meet you at Rothman's a week ago Thursday. I really enjoyed talking to you and was especially impressed by the way you could immediately go through all the verbiage right to the most important point. Your zeroing in on the joint U.S. – U.S.S.R. Peace Initiative named after Raoul Wallenberg being more important than a statue was extremely rare. The press always overlooks that point, and it is often overlooked even by people who are working with me. In general, most people find it more important to find a site for the statue of Raoul Wallenberg than to find Raoul Wallenberg. They find the statue an 'end' rather than a 'means' to keep this issue alive until it is resolved and the real project begins. It was nice talking to you!

I read in the local paper that you had an interview with a Soviet journalist. Although I know the press can be misleading, I did feel that you had a very good attitude towards the Soviets. You did a great job!"

Things were going well….for a while.

Chapter Twenty-Three
The Swan Club

In spring 1990, I continued working on trying to get the Washington Resolutions amended and passed, to request an impartial investigation. I tried to influence the Swedes to release their information on alleged sightings of Raoul Wallenberg in Soviet prisons. By this time, I also had back-up legislation in Albany duplicating the Washington Resolutions, just in case they did not pass.

The Resolution in Washington was in the House Foreign Affairs Committee, chaired by Congressman Dante Fascell of Florida. It was also in several House sub-committees: Europe and the Middle East, chaired by Congressman Lee Hamilton of Indiana; Human Rights and International Organizations, chaired by Congressman Gus Yatron of Pennsylvania; and International

Relations, chaired by Congressman Mervyn Dymally of California. This was in addition to the Senate Foreign Affairs Committee, chaired by Senator Pell, for a total of five Committees, and Committee Chairmen in Washington. There was also a Wallenberg Resolution in Albany at the same time.

There was someone on nightly TV saying "It's 11 o'clock. Do you know where your children are?" I said to myself all the time "It's 11 o'clock. Do you know where your Resolutions are?"

Assemblyman Tom DiNapoli had an interesting suggestion. His letter to me said in part,

"Thank you for your recent letters. It's always good to hear from you.

First, let me state clearly that you have in no way imposed upon our relationship or our friendship. It's been a great honor to work with you on behalf of the Raoul Wallenberg cause and I appreciate your patience in understanding the impossible pressures of my schedule.

Secondly, with regard to the Swedish and Soviet versions of the Wallenberg case, that presents a difficult proposition. The history of world politics since World War II no doubt colors the differences in these two versions. Even with the recent changes, old attitudes obviously persist. I feel that your efforts, on a Long Island level, have contributed much to the increased openness on the part of the Soviets regarding this issue. The best suggestion I might have for you to further your efforts might be for an expanded dialogue involving not only the Soviet UN officials but also Swedish UN officials. Perhaps one of the future programs of the Long Island Committee can include a joint Swedish/Soviet panel to address the Raoul Wallenberg case."

My next event was a party at the Swan Club in Roslyn Harbor, one of the loveliest venues on the North Shore of Long Island!

This was a donated party. The Swan Club gave me the party. Wasn't that nice of them!

The way I was lucky enough to get the party went like this... Every evening I walked my dog, Danny, a golden retriever mix, in Sea Cliff. We usually walked on Sea Cliff Avenue. One evening while walking Danny on Sea Cliff Avenue, I passed The Coalition to Save Hempstead Harbor office. Their fund raiser, Marie Sisko was inside. I went in.

Marie had called my home to request that my daughter, Marisa, who had volunteered for her previously, come in again. Marisa was in Baldwin with her Dad. I stopped in to tell Marie.

Somehow we started talking, became friends, and ultimately Marie Sisko was able to persuade Stan Shapiro, owner of the Swan Club to donate a cocktail party to me. Thank you Marie! Thank you Stan!

I invited everyone: Soviet officials, Swedish officials, County elected officials, State Elected officials, Federal Legislators, founders of other Wallenberg Committees: Norma Anderson of the Jamestown Raoul Wallenberg Committee, and Leona Feldman of the Philadelphia Raoul Wallenberg Committee, the Jewish and Christian communities, members of the Scandinavian Accordion Club group, family and friends, and the general public through press releases, to a party at the Swan Club in Roslyn.

The overt reason for the cocktail party was raising funds for a statue of Raoul Wallenberg. The covert reason was to influence Senator Moynihan to amend Resolution S. Con. Res. 60 to seek an impartial investigation of Raoul Wallenberg in the Soviet Union, and pass it. Then we would know once and for all, the fate of Raoul Wallenberg.

Both the Swedish diplomats – Arne Thoren and Sten Ericsson, and the Soviet diplomats – Demetri Bykov and Boris Tsepov, attended the party. Neither pair wanted to sit with the other. They preferred to sit on opposite sides of the room. I needed a dialogue. I needed to have them sitting together. This is where being a woman pays off. A man would not have been able to do this. I gently, almost imperceptibly, linked arms with these men. Then gently, again, almost imperceptivity, I pulled them to where I wanted them.

The net result was a dialogue where the Swedes maintained that Raoul Wallenberg was alive in Soviet prison, and the Soviets maintained that they did not have him.

Letters were read from Senator Moynihan and Congressman Mrazek which said in part:

"Raoul Wallenberg was one of this century's enduring moral giants. It is most appropriate that you have gathered to pay tribute to his historic role in saving tens of thousands of lives during the waning days of the holocaust." (Senator Moynihan)

"Please excuse my absence tonight and accept my best wishes to all those in attendance.

I take great pride in the work that you have done with the Raoul Wallenberg Committee of Long Island. Your organization has helped to educate not only the public, but officials at all levels of government, to the importance of the cause of Raoul Wallenberg.

Although the Soviet Union has undergone profound changes, it is important that we never relax our efforts in the United States toward learning the truth about a great humanitarian. I am pleased to have sponsored the legislation in the 101st Congress calling on the Soviets to release all available records of Raoul Wallenberg. I will work hard to insure that this legislation receives the attention it deserves.

I also applaud your efforts to build a statue of Raoul Wallenberg here on Long Island and I stand ready to assist in any way possible.

I am confident the Raoul Wallenberg Committee of Long Island will continue to provide great leadership for many years to come. Best wishes for continued success.

Sincerely, (Bob) Robert J. Mrazek Member of Congress"

Besides members of the Raoul Wallenberg Committee of Long Island, the Swedish group, and others, representatives of Nassau County Republican Chairman Joseph Mondello, and New York State Senator Ralph Marino attended.

We had a wonderful evening with Swedish accordion music, food, drinks, and dancing. Steve Berman took terrific photos of the

Swedish and Soviet diplomats, as well as the other Wallenberg Committee Presidents.

In my thank you letter to Bob Mrazek I wrote:

"I am enclosing pictures of the April 25, 1990 event at the Swan Club. The Swedish Consul, Sten Ericsson attended as well as the Soviet Chief of Legal Affairs, Boris Tsepov and Soviet Deputy Demitri Bykov. Also attending were the Presidents of the Wallenberg Committees in Philadelphia and Jamestown, New York.

Also seen in one picture is my daughter Marisa (13) who thought you lived in the mobile office. I wrote to you several years ago and mentioned it in a letter. You seemed to enjoy that comment. She is the one with hair pulled back from her ear. My other daughter, Becky is also in the picture to the far left with her boyfriend. Yes, there was also a room full of adults not shown in the picture.

Thank you for your letter and for sending Martha. She sat at the table with both the representatives of Chairman Joseph Mondello and State Senator Ralph Marino. I'll leave the rest to your imagination.

The Swedes and Soviets did not talk to each other about Wallenberg. However, the Swede told me that Wallenberg is alive and hope for his release. The Soviets again told me they want more than anything to release him but they can't.

Please amend the legislation to seek an impartial investigation of all alleged sightings of Mr. Wallenberg in Soviet prison since 1947. This is not an issue from the past, it is an issue which impacts on the future. In a nuclear age, it is necessary to remove all unnecessary mistrust. The U.S. has a responsibility in this matter since they initiated Wallenberg's mission.

I know you are working hard on the existing legislation, so am I. I have visited

Senator Pell, spoke to the staff of the House Committee and Sub-Committee Chairpeople and asked some of their (out of state) constituents to send letters. I am also mailing them all pictures of the Swan Club event.

You can be sure of one thing, that the memory of Raoul Wallenberg and what he stands for will never disappear while you and other responsible legislators continue to lend their support to this issue. I am looking forward to the phone call from your office saying you will do it.

Many thanks!"

I sent a similar thank you letter to Senators Moynihan and Pell, the other elected officials who participated, and, of course, Stan Shapiro who made this event possible. I also sent photos to the Swedish and Soviet diplomats who attended, and received back a thank you letter from Soviet official, Boris Tsepov. I sent letters and photos to the

Chairmen of the Committees in Washington where my legislation was, asking them to amend and pass the Resolution. They were: Congressman Lee Hamilton, Chairman of the House Foreign Affairs Committee, and House Foreign Affairs Sub-Committee Chairman: Congressman Gus Yaltron, Congressman Mervyn Dimale, and Congressman Dante Fascell, as well as Long Island Congressmen Norman Lent, Raymond McGrath, Thomas Downey, George Hochenbruchner, and James Scheuer, asking for their support.

The most important goal was realized. I had photos of the dialogue with the Swedes and the Soviets to send to Senator Moynihan. The implied message was, "I'm doing this here. What are you doing there?"

It worked!

Chapter Twenty-Four: Lobbying

The Legislative Resolutions in Washington, H. Con. Res. 165 and S. Con. Res. 60, needed to be amended. They were asking for the release of Wallenberg's prison records. Since this had already been accomplished, new Resolutions needed to ask for an impartial investigation. Hopefully, this would end all the unsubstantiated rumors that Wallenberg was alive in a Soviet prison. There was work to be done!

First there was another meeting with Senator Pell, Chairman of the Senate Foreign Relations Committee in Washington. In the follow up letter dated March 1, 1990, I wrote:

"Dear Senator Pell,

Thank you very much for meeting with me yesterday. It was a very exciting opportunity for me!

Thank you again for the interest you have taken in Resolution S. 60. Your interest has been extremely helpful!

Enclosed are a few articles published in the Soviet media about Raoul Wallenberg. They were sent to me by the Soviet officials in New York. I cannot stress enough how co-operative they have been. They have met with me many, many times. I sincerely believe that nothing would make them happier than to be able to release Raoul Wallenberg! In a time of warming US-USSR relations it would be sad to continue the past bitterness against the Soviet Union, if unwarranted.

It is my hope that the Wallenberg Resolution S. 60 will be amended and voted on as soon as possible. It is also my hope that the Swedish government will release all the information they have concerning alleged sightings of Mr. Wallenberg for Soviet investigation. Nancy (Nancy Stetson, Senator Pell's Aide) mentioned that you could suggest this to the Swedish Ambassador. I plan to invite the Swedish and Soviet Ambassadors from the U.N. to my next event. We will try to create a dialogue on this issue at that time.

No one benefits by leaving the issue of Raoul Wallenberg's whereabouts unresolved. It is a continuing heartache for all those concerned individuals who care about Mr. Wallenberg. It is a lack of responsibility on the part of the United States government not to follow up on the fate of their War Refugee Board representative. Additionally, in a nuclear age with such excellent prospects for world peace, it is an injustice to encourage unnecessary animosity.

Please continue to remain interested in resolving this issue. It is important! It can be resolved!

My very best wishes! Sharon Wallenberg"

Again, Senator Moynihan, my Senator, and sponsor of the Resolution was contacted. I am sure that photos of the Swan Club event with both Swedish and Soviet officials together was a very big help.

Congressman Dante Fascell had stated that member interest in the Resolution was necessary. To this end, I contacted New York Congressmen for support. They were Congressmen Lent, Weiss, Scheuer, McGrath, Downey, and Hochbruchner.

Congressman Norman Lent responded,

"Dear Ms. Wallenberg,

Thank you for your most recent correspondence on the fate of Raoul Wallenberg and the need for an impartial investigation of his disappearance in the Soviet prison system.

As one who has long been active in the effort to uncover more information from the Soviets on Raoul Wallenberg, I would certainly welcome a scrupulous and thorough investigation. Per your request, I have contacted Chairman Dante Fascell of the Foreign Affairs Committee to request his assistance in moving forward legislation in support of such an inquiry.

Enclosed please find a copy of my letter to Chairman Fascell. If I can be of any further assistance in this matter, please do not hesitate to contact me. Once again, thank you for staying in touch.

With warm regards, I remain Sincerely,

Norman F. Lent, Member of Congress"

In his letter to Chairman Dante B. Fascell, Congressman Lent wrote in part:

"As you know, the Soviet Union claims that Raoul Wallenberg died of a heart attack in a Soviet prison in 1947. However, the Soviets have never produced his remains or any convincing evidence to verify his death. In fact, rumors persist that he is still alive in Soviet custody.

Recently, I was contacted by Ms. Sharon Wallenberg whose organization, the Raoul Wallenberg Committee of Long Island, strongly supports amending House Concurrent Resolution 165 to call for an impartial investigation of all alleged sightings of Raoul Wallenberg since 1947. I can certainly appreciate the need for such an inquiry and hope that the House will have an early opportunity to support one.

For your review, I am enclosing copies of letters I have received from Ms. Wallenberg. I hope that you will take her strong feelings in this matter to heart.

Sincerely, Norman F. Lent, Member of Congress"

Congressman Lent also wrote the same letter to Congressman Lee Hamilton, House Foreign Affairs Sub-Committee Chairman.

Congressman Gus Yatron, Chairman of the House Subcommittee on Human Rights and International Organizations was extremely helpful. This was no doubt due to pressure from Leona Feldman of the Philadelphia Wallenberg Committee.

The most important of all the Congressmen was Bob Mrazek, my Congressman, and sponsor of my Resolution. He met with Sub-Committee Chairmen, Lee Hamilton, Gus Yaltron, and Mervyn Dymally to discuss the Resolution. Ultimately it was his responsibility. I did my best to try to help Bob with this big job.

Personally, I think that the difficulty was the fact that there are so many Congressmen. I came to call the United States House of

Representatives the "Mad House". It became surrealistically complicated simply because there were so many of them. There was that, and the sabotage.

Chapter Twenty-Five:
Lee Hamilton

An important part of lobbying is finding a way to motivate an otherwise unresponsive legislator. The best way to do this is usually through the elected official's district. Congressman Lee Hamilton, Chairman of the Europe and the Middle East Subcommittee, presented this challenge. I needed to find a way to influence Lee Hamilton through his district in Indiana.

In the spring of 1990, I had the opportunity to represent Amnesty International Group 17, Great Neck, at the Amnesty International Annual Meeting at Boston University. The Great Neck group gave me some money for gas from its treasury, and I drove to Boston. I stayed with a member of U.S. Servas, a Peace organization I belonged to, and later represented at the United Nations. I brought some coffee cake that I had purchased in a bakery on Long Island to eat. I am a budget traveler.

My main concern was Congressman Lee Hamilton, Chairman of the Europe and the Middle East House Sub Committee. I had even brought a poster made by the Peace and Justice Committee of my Church, Saint Boniface, Martyr, Sea Cliff. The poster asked for constituents of Lee Hamilton. I displayed it at the Amnesty International plenary session.

Next, I attended meetings on issues important to members of the Amnesty International Group 17 in Great Neck. At the first meeting, the speaker asked me if I was from Indiana. The lack of sleep from the previous night, and my obsession with Lee Hamilton made me feel like the word "Indiana" was written on my forehead. I said "Yes". So did the woman next to me. I had chosen to sit next to her because she seemed like a nice person. Obviously I was not from Indiana, and corrected myself. She was from Indiana!

After the meeting, we walked to the Boston University cafeteria together for lunch. There was a woman waving to us from a table. I could hardly believe my good luck! Two of them were from Indiana!

I told Sandra Alleyne and Susan Labaj the story of Raoul Wallenberg, which distracted them from the fact that I only had a piece of cake from Long Island for lunch. The other woman told me the two main employers in Lee Hamilton's District are Arvin Industries and Cummins Engine. I wrote that down. They also told me the word Houser, and told me it was derogatory.

I left Boston as soon as possible after the Amnesty events. I was anxious to get back to Long Island, and the C.W. Post, Long Island University business library. There I looked up all the officers of both companies, and wrote individual letters to all of them.

All I had was an electric typewriter. There were no personal computers for personal use in those days. I typed each letter individually to perhaps 20 officers in each company.

Arvin Industries wrote back and essentially said that their Congressman, Lee Hamilton, knew what he was doing. They did not want to interfere.

Martha Lamkin, President of the Cummins Engine Foundation, also wrote back. Her letter said in part:

"The plight of Raoul Wallenberg has touched the hearts of many. Certainly, such acknowledged heroism in the face of personal risk during World War II is an example of courage to us all.

Our contacts with Congressman Hamilton's office assure us that he and his subcommittee are well aware of your concern and that attention will continue to be placed on this quest for the truth."

My letter in response said in part:

"Thank you very much for your letter and your efforts on behalf of Raoul Wallenberg. I received my first letter from Congressman Hamilton yesterday. I have been writing to him for months but amazingly it was after your interest that he wrote to me."

From then on, whenever I wanted Lee Hamilton to do something, I overnight mailed to Martha Lamkin. Suddenly Lee found whatever it was I wanted him to do on his desk. Thank you, Ms. Lamkin, and the ladies from Indiana!

Chapter Twenty-Six: Lantos vs. Ackerman

There was intense lobbying involved to amend and pass, House Concurred Resolution 165 (H. Con. Res. 165) to seek an impartial investigation of the disappearance of Raoul Wallenberg, introduced at my request. It became apparent that the legislation had an adversary in Congress. Congressman Dante Fascell, Chairman of the House Foreign Relations Committee, wanted to involve Congressman Tom Lantos.

Congressman Fascell's letter to Congressman Lent dated June 4, 1990 said in part:

"That resolution is pending before three subcommittees of the Committee on Foreign Affairs. I appreciate the deep concern of the Wallenberg family and others about this issue and would hope that as United States –

Soviet relations improve, our ability to get to the bottom of this case and find out what happened to Mr. Wallenberg improve.

My colleague on the Committee, Mr. Lantos of California, has had a keen interest in, and commitment to, this issue. I intend to work with him and others to insure that everything we can do is done to resolve this case. I will also check with the subcommittees involved to determine what plans they have for this resolution. This important case has languished too long, and an inquiry into the case is appropriate.

Thank you for your letter. With best regards, I am Sincerely yours, Dante B. Fascell, Chairman Committee of Foreign Affairs"

With the involvement of Tom Lantos, the House Resolution was sure to fail – which it ultimately did.

Lantos met with the Swedish relatives before they went to Moscow in October

1989 to receive Raoul Wallenberg's prison records and personal items. Lantos directed them to Senator Moynihan and Congressman Mrazek to ask them to stop work on the Resolutions, H. Con. Res. 165, and S. Con. Res. 60. Initially Moynihan and Mrazek did stop their efforts. The involvement of Tom Lantos in the Resolution he had already tried to derail, would insure its failure.

As far as I was concerned, this was a Long Island issue. The actions that were resolving the issue of Raoul Wallenberg started in GLEN COVE, not Budapest. I recruited Congressman Gary Ackerman from Queens and Long Island, who was on the House Foreign Affairs Committee. Gary was willing to be objective with the Swedish and Soviet viewpoints. I suggested to House Foreign Affairs Committee Chairman Dante Fascell that Congressman Ackerman, not Congressman Lantos, be in charge of the Resolution. I also asked Congressmen

Mrazek and Lent to work with Congressman Ackerman on the House Foreign Affairs Committee to make this a nice little Long Island threesome.

In my letter to Congressman Lent I wrote in part,

"Please keep your eye on this legislation for me. In have been hearing all good things about you from everywhere – the North Shore and the South Shore, the Democrats and the Republicans. I have enjoyed receiving the letters and articles with your little card and handwritten messages."

Working with Congressman Ackerman was fun! The staffer I spoke to was Arthur Flug. I called Arthur so many times that I even embarrassed myself. I apologized to Arthur. "I'm sorry to be a pest". "You're not a pest, Sharon. If you were a pest, I would tell them to say I'm not here", he said. I guess that's a compliment. Every time in I went to see Arthur, he always let me sit in Gary's chair.

By August 1990, the Resolution to seek an impartial investigation of the disappearance of Raoul Wallenberg had passed out of three House Foreign Affairs Sub-Committees, and had come into the full House Foreign Affairs Committee for a vote, but was never voted on.

Chapter Twenty-Seven:
New York State Resolution

The Wallenberg Resolutions seeking an impartial investigation that were introduced, at my request, were 'cooking' in Washington. As a back-up, I asked Assemblyman Tom DiNapoli and New York State Senator Norman Levy to also introduce Resolutions to seek an impartial investigation. These Resolutions were having ups and downs in Albany due to the never ending ordeals over the State budget.

At around that time, I went for a rather routine visit to Congressman Mrazek's office in Huntington. I learned that Senator Claiborne Pell may be having a tough Senate race. I wrote to him immediately to let him know that I, and people in my Church, were praying for him. I told him that he was a pivotal person in the work I had done on behalf of Raoul Wallenberg, and that every time I read a Legislative

Update from Peace Organizations, his name was always mentioned. I didn't think there was anyone else like him! I sent gratitude, admiration, prayers, and best wished for his success. He thanked me for my particularly nice, thoughtful letter and said that my kind words were much appreciated.

It would sometimes become very overwhelming to be doing everything simultaneously, while also working, paying bills, and dealing with personal situations. Sometimes I don't know how I did it!

Chapter Twenty-Eight: Senate Resolution Passes!

On June 7, 1990, the amended United States Senate version of the Resolution: Senate Concurrent Resolution 60 (S. Con. Res. 60) seeking an impartial investigation of the disappearance of Raoul Wallenberg passed out of the full Senate in Washington! The Resolution had the signatures of one hundred United States Senators on it! To this day, I think this is one of the greatest achievements of my life. And I did it all from the little 100+ year old fixer-upper house in Sea Cliff, with nothing to work with except imagination and determination!

Chapter Twenty Nine: Speak Softly and Carry a Big Stick

There is no point in accomplishing something in Washington or Albany unless it can get results. This does not happen in a vacuum. In order to be effective, the Resolution, which passed out of the full Senate with the signatures of one hundred United States Senators needed to be presented to the Soviet Union.

A Garden Party Concert at the Museum-In-The-Park Garden in Eisenhower Park was the scene of the Raoul Wallenberg's Birthday Celebration on Saturday, August 4, 1990. Swedish and Soviet diplomats, as well as U.S. elected officials, and the general public were invited.

Music filled the air from the harp – flute duo of Karen Strass and Katherine Battel, noted local performers. Ms. Strauss is the founding Director of the Long Island Harp Ensemble, and Ms. Battel played with the Massapequa Philharmonic and Massapequa based Woodwind Quintet.

Guests were served birthday cake and punch. Elegance was the keynote – from linen clad tables to the sparkle of silver and crystal vases of flowers from Long Island gardens.

It was fun deciding on the location for the event riding in a golf cart with Nassau County Parks Department employee Kevin O'Donnell. I chattered away until finally he said in desperation, "Sharon, don't tell me who you called!" I didn't realize just how naturally I managed to maneuver past obstacles that were not a common occurrence for most people.

Only the Soviet diplomats attended. The Swedes were not able to attend due to last minute problems. Letters were read from

Senator Daniel Patrick Moynihan, Congressman Robert Mrazek, Congressman Gary Ackerman, Town Supervisor Joseph Mondello, Nassau County Democratic County Committee Chairman John Matthews. Carol Siegel represented the Jewish community, and Barbara Bixby represented the Swedish community. The Catholic Diocese of Rockville Centre sent a representative.

It was good to see Soviet diplomat Demetri Bykov again. He had nice things to say about General Eisenhower, his contemporary and the park's namesake. I spoke softly and sweetly to Mr. Bykov. I suggested that there should be an impartial investigation including Swedes, Soviets, and Americans. He politely declined with, "No, that's not a good idea."

I felt sorry for him, and the Soviets, because they had already gone above and beyond what should have been required. Unfortunately, this was the only way to end the sensationalism, false claims, and let Raoul Wallenberg rest in peace.

I was carrying a "big stick" – the United States Senate Resolution seeking an impartial investigation, with the signatures of one hundred United State Senators on it. I gave it to Mr. Bykov along with the New York State Resolution by Assemblyman DiNapoli and State Senator Norman Levy which passed. I knew that left the Soviet Union with no choice. With the Resolution, I gave Mr. Bykov this letter

"Dear Demetri,

This is a copy of the Resolution that passed in the United States Senate. It is the original Resolution that was prepared in Bob Mrazek's office a year ago last Spring to request the release of the prison records. It was amended this past winter in Senator Moynihan's office to seek an impartial investigation. Both times I added, deleted, negotiated, compromised, etc. The final version is not perfect, but it is not really that bad either. It was a lot of work!

The Resolution in the House of Representatives is exactly the same, but will take longer to pass because there are more people in the House and more Committees. Eventually the Resolution will pass in the House and go to the President. If he fails to create an investigating committee, Senator Moynihan will introduce new legislation that will do it.

Eventually the sensationalism will end, Soviet credibility will be restored, and we can begin to work on a joint U.S.- U.S.S.R. Peace initiative named after Raoul Wallenberg. We are making progress!"

The only way to end the sensationalism surrounding Raoul Wallenberg is to have an impartial investigation. This should forever end the myth that he is alive in a Soviet prison, as some people still believe. The Soviet Union has already done an excellent job of investigating all alleged "sightings". They also allowed the Swedes access to anything they wanted in October 1989. The last thing the Soviet Union wants is to do this all over again. However, without a neutral third party, in this case, the Americans, it was still "he said – she said".

I stressed to Mr. Bykov that there needs to be neutral Americans involved to be objective about the findings so this can end once and for all. I really hoped this would be the end.

I thanked Parks Commissioner John Kiernan for the use of that very cute section of Eisenhower Park, and for stopping by to see if we needed anything, which was a nice touch. I thanked Hubie for the great birthday cake, the musicians, and all the supporters who provided linens, flatware, crystal, and flowers.

My thank you to my Congressman, Bob Mrazek said in part:

"Thank you very much for sending Ken (Schwitz) to the event in Eisenhower Park. He made a statement which sounded like we were in a mutual admiration society. He really has been instrumental to me during the past – would you believe – year and a half. It is so nice to know that he has kind feelings for me and does not regard me as a giant imposition.

It was so touching to receive your generous donation. This reminds me of the story 'The Magi's Gift'. Do you remember that one? I just gave you a donation for your Campaign and now you made a donation back to me.

You may not be aware of it, but I spoke to Ruth McKay about volunteering for your Campaign. She told me to wait. I just want you to know that if you need a satisfied constituent to help with your Campaign, I would be more than happy to help."

Of course, I thanked all the other elected officials, and everyone else who participated. On August 5, 1990, I sent the following letter to Soviet Official Demetri Bykov, and by extension to the Soviet Union:

"Dear Demetri,

"It was good to see you on Saturday, and I can appreciate your concerns.

I know how important it is to have closer relations between the U.S. and the U.S.S.R. As you know, I was very pleased with the joint U.S. – U.S.S.R. statement on Kuwait. It is my ultimate goal to have the joint Peace initiative you mentioned named on behalf of Raoul Wallenberg. It is my further hope that the reduced tensions between our two nations will translate into better conditions in the entire world. It is specifically the people in the Third World who I would hope to benefit from this since they most closely resemble the innocent victims that Raoul Wallenberg saved during World War II.

The Raoul Wallenberg issue is indeed a very small issue when viewed in a world-wide context. However, for whatever reasons, Wallenberg is something of a phenomenon that cannot be dealt with in ordinary terms.

Do you remember when I suggested that an American go to the meeting in Moscow last October? It was because I hoped that would provide an impartial account of what happened. The Swedish relatives went to Washington before going to Moscow and asked Bob Mrazek not to send an American. They also asked his office in Washington not to tell the office in New York who had made this request. I found out through a phone call I received from someone else. It would make sense, however since they were in Washington having their pictures taken and being honored at a dinner with Congressman Tom Lantos.

The relatives further convinced Bob Mrazek that they would be returning with Raoul Wallenberg. Did you know that? Naturally they reported their disappointment. Bob was livid. He wouldn't do any more work for me. At first I didn't believe the released records were accurate. I changed my mind after meeting with you and Vladimir. Unfortunately, not everyone has the opportunity that I have had. Many people expect to someday meet Mr. Wallenberg, including Carol Siegel. Did you hear her say that?

I do not think it is possible to move on to have a joint peace initiative until everyone agrees about the fate of this outstanding person.

I know the Soviet Union has been extremely cooperative. The problem has been on the Swedish side. You said that they were distraught. Unfortunately, these distraught people are able to influence world opinion. It ignites the former bitterness.

There are times in everyone's life when they encounter a situation that they cannot handle alone. That is what friends are for. Please let the United States help you. The United States initiated Wallenberg's mission, and has a responsibility to resolve it. As soon as this is over we will have a stronger foundation for a peace initiative.

When Mrazek and Moynihan stopped working for me last fall, I went to Senator D'Amato. (This is probably who you thought Tom DiNapoli was when you first met him and called him "Senator"). I finally was able to involve Senator Pell. He was not at all anxious to become involved but I gave him a push. He was the one who got Mrazek and Moynihan to work for me again, and pushed the legislation through.

I don't know if you know what you are up against with these distraught people, and how entrenched their influence is.

Please let the United States help you in dealing with this extremely difficult and delicate situation. Simply let a few kind-hearted Americans see the same little list of things to investigate that you had last fall, and let them report facts, not sensationalism. It will be over very fast. It is similar to childbirth. No one wants to go through that pain, but there is no other way, and once it is over there is a beautiful child, and the unpleasant memories are gone.

I noticed how sensitive you were when George Gach mentioned he was a slave laborer after World War II. George did not expect to speak, and just said a few things about his life which were true without being prepared. As you could see, he has no bitterness. Did you notice the photographer from Newsday? He was black, and I wouldn't be surprised if his great-grandparents were slaves. They were not slaves for a few months, or a few years, but all of their lives.

This country was conceived in the blood of the Indians. It was built on their rape, robbery, and murders. In its adolescence it had a slave trade totally devoid of any semblance of morality or humanitarianism. In young adulthood, it was the only nation to explode a nuclear bomb – after the Japanese navy was no longer a threat. As we know, it deserted its Soviet ally. In more recent times, we had Americans in Asia killing Asians. I lived through that, and still do not understand why that had to happen.

Please do not ever be embarrassed about anything from your nation's past. You may not realize it but this nation is the most violent on earth. There couldn't be anything worse than this! Don't worry about the past, let's go forward from here and build a better future.

I know you would love to disregard the unpleasant aspect of an investigation. I know at times you perceive it as a lack of appreciation of Soviet co-operation. That is not my motivation at all.

My Congressman is a good and honest person, and I am extremely loyal to him. However for this work I have selected Congressman Gary Ackerman. He is open and willing. Congress ended at 2 am and my event was at 1 pm on the same day. His office is trying very hard to set aside some time in his schedule. I think he is the right person to involve in the details of this little undertaking. It will be protection for the U.S.S.R. from distraught people, the Jewish press, and other sources of sensationalism igniting any former bitterness. I wish sometimes that Raoul Wallenberg could be a little more ordinary, but I really think this case is more unusual, requires a little more work, but will be more than worth it in the end.

All I have to do is pick up the telephone in my house in Sea Cliff and a call a Glen Cove phone number and get Ken, who you met Saturday, and say I want the legislation to stop. It is possible that I will get a message back that it can't be done, but I doubt it. Shall I make that phone call?

Every good wish, Sharon".

Then the impartial investigation began.

Valentin Lozinskily, Sharon Wallenberg,
Sand Point Flute Concert January 1990

Reception Conversation between Author
Rabbi Frederick Werbell and Soviet
Officials Dimitry Bykov and Valentin
Lozinskiy

Demetry Rachmanov, Piano and Helene
Derwinger, Flute

Sands Point Flute Concert Audience
including Soviets Valentin Lozinsky,
Dimitry Bykov, Sharon Wallenberg's
Daughters, Marisa Brown, Rebekah Brown
and their friends Astrid, John, and Claire.

Carol Shapiro Siegel, American Jewish
Congress, Sharon Wallenberg, Laura Silver
in back and Mark Golden.

Swan Club Cocktail Reception April 1990.
Soviet Official Dimitry Bykov, Swedish
Official Sten Ericsson, Sharon Wallenberg,
Swedish Official Arne Thoren.

Standing: Leona Feldman, Philadelphia Wallenberg Committee, Soviet Official Dimitry Bykov, Norma Anderson, Jamestown, N.Y. Wallenberg Committee. Seated: Swedish official Sten Ericsson, S Sharon Wallenberg, Swedish Official Arne Thoren.

Presentation of the United States Senate
Legislative Resolution Requesting an
Impartial Investigation of Raoul
Wallenberg's Disappearance in the Soviet
Union To Soviet Representative Demetri
Bykov at Eisenhower Park in August 1990.

Woman's Campaign for Probe Of Diplomat's Fate Pays Off

By Ellen Braitman

Sharon Wallenberg has been trying for nine years to learn more about the disappearance of Swedish diplomat Raoul Wallenberg, who helped save the lives of up to 100,000 Hungarian Jews during World War II.

Yesterday, she came one step closer to seeing an impartial committee investigate his apparent death in a Soviet prison 43 years ago.

Sharon Wallenberg, a Sea Cliff resident who is no relation to the diplomat, became interested in Raoul Wallenberg about 10 years ago after reading about him in a newspaper. She founded the Raoul Wallenberg Committee on Long Island and tries to raise interest in building a memorial in his honor on the Island.

Yesterday, she presented a Soviet official with a copy of pending federal legislation that calls for an impartial investigation of all alleged sightings of Raoul Wallenberg since July 17, 1947.

Upon receiving a copy of the bill, Demtri Bykov, deputy permanent representative of the Soviet Union to the United Nations, said it is important to honor "the memory of Raoul Wallenberg," who "saved so many innocent lives."

And an aide to Rep. Robert Mrazek (D-Centerport), Ken Schwitz, told the group of 35 people gathering in Eisenhower Park to celebrate Wallenberg's 78th birthday that obstacles have been cleared for the legislation to come for a vote in the House. The Senate has already approved its own version of the bill.

During the war, Raoul Wallenberg distributed thousands of protective Swedish passports, placed Jews in safe houses draped with Swedish flags and is said to have taken people right off trains headed for death camps. He disappeared in January, 1945, after driving to meet a representative of Soviet troops who liberated Hungary from the Nazis. In the years since he disappeared, Soviet officials have insisted to relatives and acquaintances that Wallenberg died of a heart attack in 1947 in Lubyanka prison, a notorious jail run by the KGB, the Soviet secret police. Last October, the Soviet government turned over Wallenberg's passport, notebooks and identity card to his relatives and apologized for his arrest by Soviet troops.

Although the Soviets say Wallenberg died 43 years ago, some Wallenberg supporters insist he could still be alive and living in a Soviet prison. Sharon Wallenberg, who has lobbied for years to get the federal legislation passed, said an impartial investigation would lay to rest questions of his life and death.

"It's necessary to end the controversy," she said. "It's necessary to know one way or another what happened." She called the Soviets "my biggest supporters" in her quest.

Bykov said every effort is being made by the Soviet Union "to investigate all the particulars, all the facts, to verify the fate of Raoul Wallenberg, who died in 1947."

Chapter Thirty: Impartial Investigation

For the first time since 1917, KGB files were opened to the public. Needless to say, there was no shortage of people willing to take the credit for this. Also, as might be expected, there were still those who considered the results inconclusive.

As usual, the Swedish and Soviet versions did not agree. An American academic, who was involved in the investigation, was heavily committed to the Swedes. The Swedes were more than willing to get their version out without releasing anything to support their claims.

The Soviets picked up the tab for the visitors' expenses. This made me sad because they had internal economic problems, and didn't deserve this additional financial burden. Ultimately, there was no real closure at that point.

Chapter Thirty-One: Impartial Investigation Results Meeting

The impartial investigation of the whereabouts of Raoul Wallenberg in the Soviet Union was very impressive. There were Soviet members of the team. The Soviets provided a staff. Equipment was provided by the Swedish government. Records, documents, files, entire prisons were opened. KGB files and archives not allowed to foreigners were opened. The investigation looked fair and complete. The Swedes took over 100,000 records back to Stockholm.

The investigation produced no evidence to support the claim that Raoul Wallenberg was alive in prison after 1947. Still the Swedish relatives and Swedish government insisted that Wallenberg was alive. The relatives insisted that Wallenberg is in a "camp of silence", although these things no longer existed. The Soviets said that the relatives were distraught.

On January 17, 1991, the Raoul Wallenberg Committee in Manhattan held a meeting to discuss the results of the Soviet investigation. Sonja Sonnenfeld flew in from Stockholm to give the opening presentation. She stated that Wallenberg was alive in a "camp of silence", even though these camps no longer exist. She acknowledged the release of Wallenberg's prison records, but did not refer to the Resolutions by Assemblyman DiNapoli, Congressman Mrazek, and Senator Moynihan which precipitated it.

Marvin Makinen, an academic from Chicago, and member of the investigating team at the request of the Swedish relatives, gave a presentation at the meeting. He also believed that Wallenberg was alive, but did not give any reasons why. He discussed the equipment used and the places investigated, but did not discuss any evidence discovered. At one point he did imply that something was found which proves that Wallenberg is alive. When questioned later he said that was not the impression he meant to give. I wrote to him to ask what further information he needed to find Wallenberg. This is my letter:

"Dear Dr. Makinen:

It was nice meeting you briefly on Saturday, January 17 in New York. As I mentioned, a Resolution asking for the release of the Soviet prison records of Raoul Wallenberg was introduced into the New York State Assembly by Assemblyman Thomas DiNapoli and New York State Senate by Senator Norman Levy on January 17, 1989. It was presented by Assemblyman DiNapoli and I to the Soviet officials in New York on January 26, 1989. Guy Von Dardle called me from Switzerland after that meeting to discuss it.

In April 1989, Congressman Robert Mrazek (my Congressman) introduced the same resolution in the U.S. House of Representatives. H. Con. Res. 165 is enclosed. It was introduced by Senator Daniel Moynihan (my Senator) in the U.S. Senate in August 1989. In August the Soviets invited the Swedes to Moscow to receive the prison records. The relatives put it off the visit until October. In September the Soviet officials in New York invited me to a meeting. I attended with a representative of Senator Moynihan, because Senator Moynihan's plane from Washington could not land in New York due to an airplane accident at LaGuardia Airport. The Soviets asked that the Resolution be delayed until they had a chance to release the records.

Nina Lagergren, Guy Von Dardle, Sonja Sonnenfeld, and Per Anger stopped in Washington on their way to Moscow to see my Congressman. They requested that he

(Mrazek) not send an American to the meeting in Moscow as the Soviets had agreed to because they wanted the meeting to remain private.

After the prison records were released in October, 1989, I had the Resolution amended to request an impartial investigation of all alleged sightings of Mr. Wallenberg and to express gratitude for the Soviet co-operation. This was done by my Senator Moynihan in spring 1990. Enclosed is a copy of the amended Resolution S. Con. Res. 60. This passed the full Senate in July 1990. The investigation was conducted in the Fall 1990.

Please let me know if there is any more specific information that would be needed in regard to the investigation which has already been conducted, and looked quite impressive. The Soviets seem to have done a very thorough job.

Again, it was nice meeting you even though I was very sick with a cold and temperature. Please let me know specifically what would make you feel this investigation is complete.

Sincerely, Sharon L. Wallenberg"

There was no response.

I sent a copy of the video of the meeting to John Hymes in Congressman Norman Lent's office with a letter which said in part:

"This video will, I hope, at least show that the investigation was carried out. I hope Mr. lent will contact the Soviet Ambassador to get a complete version of the results of the investigation.

Please tell Mr. Lent thank you very much for his concern, interest and involvement and how much I appreciate his commitment to learning the truth about Mr. Wallenberg's disappearance.

This issue belongs to all humanity not just a select few, who for whatever reason, wish to control the version of this story which is presented to the world.

Again, my thanks to you and wonderful Mr. Lent.

Cordially, Sharon L. Wallenberg"

I also wrote to Guy Von Dardle in Switzerland and Nina Lagergren in Stockholm to request the results of the impartial investigation. My letter told them that I had spoken to Mr. Sporrong of the Swedish Consulate in New York. He told me that the information obtained from this investigation was in the relative's personal possession. I went on further to give an account of all the legislative efforts in the U.S. on behalf of Raoul Wallenberg, mentioning Congressmen Mrazek, Ackerman and Lent, and Senators Moynihan and Pell. I asked Nina Lagergren and Guy Von Dardle to consider sharing the results of the investigation. Raoul Wallenberg is everyone's hero, and everyone is entitled to know his fate. I thanked them.

There was no response from either of them.

I also wrote to Senators Moynihan, Pell, Bradley, and Levin as well as Congressmen Mrazek, Lent, Ackerman to say there was no evidence to support the claim that Raoul Wallenberg was alive in a Soviet prison since 1947. I informed Soviet officials Demetri Bykov and Boris Tsepov of the meeting, its results, and my actions.

Was it finally over?

Chapter Thirty-Two:
The Lent Resolution

The House Companion Resolution 165, seeking an impartial investigation of Raoul Wallenberg's disappearance, did not pass in the House of Representatives in the 101st Congress. This was attributed to the Middle East situation. Senate Concurrent Resolution 60 had passed in the full Senate. It was no doubt responsible for the investigation in 1990. Since the mystery of Raoul Wallenberg's disappearance was still considered by some to be unresolved, Congressman Norman Lent from Long Island offered to introduce a Resolution into the 102nd Congress.

In order to prevent any hurt feelings on the part of my own Congressman (who Congressman Lent was not), I wrote a letter to Bob Mrazek on January 7, 1991 which said:

"Dear Bob,

As you know, I have devoted a considerable amount of my time and energy to the issue of Raoul Wallenberg. It is so wonderful to begin to see results during this time of Glasnost. I can still remember sitting in the Soviet Mission in Manhattan several years ago with Tom DiNapoli and the NYS Legislation, telling the Soviet officials over and over that I was coming back with my Congressman. They couldn't wait to meet you! It's funny now.

With all the progress that has been made so far, I'm not sure that we all realize that this issue has not yet been resolved. It desperately needs some kind of a real ending. Even with the complete cooperation of the Soviet Union, it is not over yet.

I was so happy when you agreed to introduce this legislation in 1989. You were the first elected official in the United States to do something on the federal level to directly affect Mr. Wallenberg if alive, and learn his true fate, if deceased. There have been a lot of successes and disappointments since that time, which now seems like ages ago. We all worked very hard, and were very involved with this issue. I appreciate everything that you and your staff did to make the progress we had.

Please let Congressman Lent introduce the legislation in the 102nd Congress. Nothing could ever change the loyalty I feel for my own Congressman, but part of me is a real pragmatist, especially where this issue is concerned. By some magic, I took a person who had never even heard of Wallenberg, didn't co-sponsor the original legislation because he was too confused, and over time transformed him into the most ardent and enthusiastic supporter of this issue that I have ever seen. I don't know how this happened. It must be magic. In his position as a senior member and a member of the Republican Party, I think he is in a good position to make the much needed progress quickly. He is devoted to this issue. I don't know why.

I really wish it were possible to adequately express my feelings of gratitude for all you have done, and that I am in no way disappointed with your work. I can still remember shopping for a Senator with you. I tried, and you tried, and I tried, and I gave up. If I didn't have you, I would have had nobody. Nothing can change that.

I wish that things did not work out this way because I feel that I am deserting you. That is not my intention. I only want to move quickly while I am unsure that Glasnost will last.

Please do not be offended by my choice of Congressman Lent. Could you instead join in my happiness that a well-placed person full of zeal is ready to go! Watch out!!!

It would be so wonderful if you would co-sponsor this legislation with Congressman Lent. Would you do that? This legislation desperately needs to have your name at the top in big letters. It just would not be any good without that. Please keep your eye on the bigger picture of this legislation. You have done more than anyone else to get this issue to where it is now. Please let him finish it with your support. This still needs your usual strong support to be finished successfully.

I am looking forward to attending Town Meetings as a regular constituent. I also look forward to writing to complain about hundreds of issues. During the time of this legislation in the U.S. house, I have only complained about the murder of the six Jesuit priests in El Salvador. I did not want to complicate the fact that we were working on an issue together with other issues. This only made me feel isolated and irresponsible. I look forward to being a normal constituent again. It is such a great feeling to have a Congressman to tell your ideas to. When I worked on your campaign, I saw people who looked frustrated. I told them to call you, and I gave them the number. They were so happy. It really is important to be able to voice your opinion. Now I can do that again.

Please support Congressman Lent. He will do a good job, better than all of us could do. We are not in the position that he is in. He is blessed with tremendous enthusiasm (I don't know why). In spite of all that, I don't think this can be a success without your support.

Please don't you desert this cause.

Sincerely, Sharon L. Wallenberg"

Congressman Norman Lent's letter of January 2, 1991 to me stated in part:

"I am very pleased to hear that you are satisfied with the progress of ongoing investigations and to learn that certain KGB files have been opened for the first time. Hopefully, new light will soon be shed on the disappearance of Mr. Wallenberg.

As the 102nd Congress gets down to business, I will be doing my utmost to ensure that Raoul Wallenberg is not forgotten. I look forward to your counsel as a resolution supporting a thorough and impartial investigation into his fate is considered."

This would be the second investigation after the release of the prison records. I did not think it was necessary, but I had no choice. Congressman Lent was determined to do this, and I could not stop him.

In his February 5, 1991 letter to me, Congressman Lent says:

"I am pleased to report that I introduced the Raoul Wallenberg resolution on January 31, 1991. It has been designated House Concurrent Resolution 58.

I have been advised that you are satisfied with the Soviet Union's investigation into the Wallenberg case. As you know, I am very interested in this matter and would gladly examine any material that you feel brings to light new and important information."

Congressman Norman Lent circulated a "Dear Colleague" letter for H. Con. Res. 58 on February 11, 1991.

On May 2, 199l, I wrote to Congressman Norman Lent telling him, among other things that the draft looked good, and I would call Senator Moynihan to get things going on the Senate side.

No, it was not over yet.

Chapter Thirty-Three: An Evening of Magic

On May 1, 1991, the Raoul Wallenberg Committee of the United States held "An Evening of Magic" at the Waldorf Astoria honoring Alan "Ace" Greenberg, of Bear Stearns. The price of one ticket was more than the entire budget I had used for all my activities on behalf of Raoul Wallenberg in nearly ten years. I called Mr. Greenberg, and he was nice enough to invite me to come to the dinner, and bring a guest. I also mailed to Mr. Greenberg a list of all the legislation sponsored at my request on behalf of Raoul Wallenberg, and a summary of related activities. The guest I brought to the dinner was Joel Meisner, owner of a foundry on Long Island.

Joel had offered to help me raise funds for a statue of Raoul Wallenberg on Long Island. He said he wanted to see who was at the dinner so he would know who was interested. Marie Sisko, Fund Raiser for the Coalition To Save Hempstead Harbor, and friend, instructed me to get a list of the people attending the dinner. I was able to get a list. Almost everyone was an employee of Bear Stearns.

It was evident from the program that the Committee had tremendous financial support from both corporations, as well as wealthy individuals. In fact, the proceeds of the evening were approximately $400,000. It was a little unclear what they planned to do with the money, just "inform and inspire". I don't think they wanted any competition for fund raising from Long Island. I don't know who Joel contacted, or who contacted him. I never heard from Joel Meisner again. I tried unsuccessfully to resurrect him, but it was impossible.

Soon, it became evident that my activities to solve the mystery of Raoul Wallenberg's disappearance might end due to a lack of funds. Specifically, there was a phone disconnect notice due to all the calls to Washington, mostly to Senator Moynihan. I contacted both the Manhattan Wallenberg Committee and Mr. Greenberg to see if they would donate a modest amount so the work which was resolving the mystery of Raoul Wallenberg's disappearance could continue. I even enclosed the phone bill showing all the long distance calls were to Senator Moynihan's Washington phone number. No one responded. Eventually, a member of the Raoul Wallenberg Committee of Long Island, Brian Sauer, made a donation from his Law Firm, Shayne, Dachs, Stanici, Corker, and Sauer, in Mineola. Thank you, Brian!

Chapter Thirty-Four:
If You Can't Go Up, You Must Go Down

In the spring of 1991, the Soviets mysteriously stopped co-operating with me. There were still no published conclusive results of the impartial investigation.

While Congressman Lent wanted a second investigation, I tried to get the results of the first one. The Soviets would not respond to me, so I asked Senator Pell, Chairman of the Senate Foreign Relations Committee, to request the results. I did not think the Soviets would ignore someone of his stature, but they did.

If the Soviets were not concerned about ignoring an important U.S. Senator, maybe they would be concerned about the water and garbage pick-up for their Glen Cove residence. 'Going up' to the Chairman of the Senate Foreign Relations Committee did not work. I tried 'going down' to the Mayor of Glen Cove. I asked Glen Cove Mayor Donald De Riggi to write to the Soviets. They responded to him.

Glen Cove Mayor and Supervisor Donald P. DeRiggi wrote to Mr. Sergey N. Shestakov, Assistant to the Permanent Representative of the Union of Soviet Socialist Republic to the United Nations on April 30, 1991. This is the April 25, 1991 reply

"Dear Mr. Mayor,

With reference to your letter of March 19, 1991 concerning an inquiry as to the whereabouts of Raoul Wallenberg I would like to inform you of the following.

The fact of death of Raoul Wallenberg in 1947 is highly deplorable but indisputable, and from this standpoint any further investigation of his whereabouts are senseless. However, in the spirit of goodwill and readiness to cooperate in clarifying the fate of the late Swedish diplomat, the Soviet authorities released in 1989, during a visit to the Soviet Union of relatives of Raoul Wallenberg, all existing prison records of Mr. Wallenberg. Recently the Soviet side received a delegation of International Working Group on the fate of Raoul Wallenberg, which included, inter alia, several Soviet citizens (Mr. M. Chlenov, Chairman of the Soviet Jewish Organizations League, Mr. A. Roginsky, member of "Memorial' society and others). The group operated in the Soviet Union under the name of the 'Joint Soviet-International Commission on the Fate and Whereabouts of Raoul Wallenberg'. On the request of the Swedish side, including Mr. Wallenberg's relatives, the group was given an access to the files of the Vladimir prison – the site of alleged sightings of R. Wallenberg after 1947. Though the group has examined more than 100 thousand personal files of the former inmates of the prison, they would not, and obviously could not, find anything to substantiate their hypothesis.

As to the 'report' of this Commission, to the best of our knowledge, it was never produced and, therefore, we are not in a position to assist in obtaining a copy of it.

Very truly yours, Yuli M. Vorontsov"

I thanked Mayor De Riggi in a letter that said in part:

"It is so nice of you to continue your support of this important issue. From the first moment you joined my first demonstration at the Soviet Mission until now, you have always been an invaluable asset to this cause."

The bottom line - there was no 'report'. The Swedes examined more than 100,000 files, and could not find anything to substantiate their claims. I wrote to the Swedish Government and the relatives and asked them to release the information they were basing their claims on.

They did not respond.

Chapter Thirty-Five: Include an American

Congressman Norman Lent introduced his Resolution to seek a second impartial investigation of the disappearance of Raoul Wallenberg in the 102nd Congress. The Swedes continued to maintain that Raoul Wallenberg was alive despite an extensive first investigation. In order to prevent another impasse, I suggested including an American, preferably a Congressman from the House Foreign Affairs Committee, as an impartial third party.

I conveyed the latest events to the Soviets through Mr. Bykov. My letter of May 2, 1991 to him said:

"Dear Demetri,

It is always so nice seeing you, I regret that we don't have the opportunity to get together more often.

There is some bad news for the Soviet Union. Today I received a letter from Congressman Norman Lent. He is prepared to introduce a Resolution calling for an impartial investigation. I enclose his letter, the latest draft and the original draft. As you can see, I was able to tone down the Resolution, but I cannot stop it.

In view of the fact that the evidence is in the possession of the relatives who maintain that Wallenberg is alive and the Swedish government is not officially involved, there is no other recourse but to do it again. I regret the inconvenience this will cause. As you will see from Mr. Lent's letter, he is very determined to go through with this. I don't think I could stop him if I wanted to, and since this issue is still unresolved I am going along with him.

If you need someone in Washington to talk to and don't feel comfortable with Norman Lent, go to Gary Ackerman. He is on the House Foreign Affairs Committee where this legislation will go. I can get him put in charge of the legislation in committee. He is very open and fair. He was in Israel during the scud missile attacks. I am sure if this needs some official U.S. involvement, Mr. Ackerman is the best one for the job. I can get Mr. Lent to go along with that.

Good luck. I am sorry this couldn't be resolved easier for everyone.

Cordially, Sharon"

Senator Pell wrote to the Soviet Ambassador to request an American be part of the second impartial investigation. In his letter to Soviet Ambassador Viktor G. Komplektov dated June 18, 1991, he said:

"Dear Mr. Ambassador:

I understand that your government has begun a new investigation concerning the fate of Raoul Wallenberg.

I am very pleased to hear that, and I wish to commend the Soviet government for its willingness to reopen the Wallenberg case and settle the matter once and for all. In this connection, it occurred to me that in light of the great American interest in the Wallenberg case, it might be helpful to have an American present during the investigation. Upon completion of the investigation, that American would then be in a position to explain the results from a first-hand perspective to the interested American organization.

I would appreciate it if you would convey these thoughts to the appropriate authorities in Moscow and let me know what their reaction is.

With every good wish.

Ever sincerely, Claiborne Pell
United States Senate Committee on Foreign Relations

My response to Senator Pell on June 27, 1991 was:

"Your letter arrived today like an answer to my prayers. It brought joy and delight beyond description.

It is so wonderful to know that finally the mystery of Raoul Wallenberg will be resolved.....

Senator Pell you are like a Guardian Angel to this issue! Thanks so much for coming through again!

Warmest wishes,

Sharon L. Wallenberg"

Naturally I was anxious to share the news with my Soviet friend, which I did on June 27, 1991 in the following letter.

"Dear Demetri,

This is just to let you know that Senator Pell, Chairman of the Senate Foreign Relations Committee, wrote to the Soviet Ambassador to request an American at the Wallenberg investigation in Moscow. A copy is attached as well as a copy of my reply.

As you know, only the Swedish version of what is happening appears in the media. Enclosed is an article on the investigation from U.S. News and World Report earlier this month. I was informed by Rabbi Werbell that the information referred to in the article is a letter from Hans Lloyda who said he was imprisoned for 25 years because he sat with an important prisoner – Wallenberg. There is a grammatical error which can imply 1949 but it doesn't. This information, of course, does not appear in the press.

I really think the only way to end the sensationalism is to let sweet, caring, honest, and fair people like Senator Pell, Congressman Ackerman, Senator Moynihan and Congressman Lent (who is a little tougher) take care of this. They will be believed.

Hope everything is going well for you.

Sincerely, Sharon"

I tried to recruit an elected official from Washington or Albany to participate in the investigation. I started with Congressman Gary Ackerman, from Forest Hills, Queens and Long Island, and member of the House Foreign Affairs Committee.

My letter to Arthur Flug, District Administrator for Congressman Ackerman said:

"Dear Arthur,

Thank you very much for meeting with me today when I stopped in at your office. It is always nice to see you, and I appreciate how friendly and nice you are.

Here is the fax that I sent to the Washington office because I thought he was there. Congressman Ackerman's involvement in the transport of the Ethiopians is very impressive!

There is a second investigating committee being formed to investigate Mr. Wallenberg's disappearance. As you know, the last time there were no results, and the Swedish and Soviet positions remain the same. It appeared in the media that the investigation is not going forward, but this is not confirmed by the Swedish Consulate, Swedish Foreign Ministry or the Soviet Mission.

Please ask Congressman Ackerman to ask the Soviet Ambassador to include and American representative at that investigation. I hope Congressman Ackerman will volunteer to go, and review the results in the House Foreign Affairs Committee, and end this forever.

In the event that Congressman Ackerman is too busy to become involved, please ask him to recommend someone on the House Foreign Affairs Committee who would be willing to do it.

Thank you very much. It was good seeing you today.

Sincerely, Sharon L. Wallenberg"

It looked like final closure was right around the corner! But it wasn't!

Chapter Thirty-Six: Ackerman, Lent, and Pell Stop Involvement

On October 6, 1991, the Swedish Consul General, Arne Thoren, gave a presentation at the Raoul Wallenberg Humanitarian Award ceremony. It was an inflammatory speech alleging Soviet lack of transparency, and claiming that Raoul Wallenberg was still alive in Soviet prison.

I asked for a copy of the speech the Consul General had read from, immediately after his presentation. Unfortunately, during that less than a split second, the speech was 'lost'. Brian Sauer, who had accompanied me to the ceremony, wrote to the Swedish Consul General:

"Dear General Consul Thoren:

It was a great pleasure meeting you at the 1991 Raoul Wallenberg Humanitarian

Award presentation on 6 October, 1991. Your kind words about Raoul Wallenberg, one who holds a special place in all of our hearts, moved us deeply.

Our Committee would appreciate it if you would send us a copy of your speech. We hope you were able to retrieve it before leaving the art gallery. Allow me to take this opportunity to thank you in advance for your courtesy in sending us a copy.

Respectfully,

The Raoul Wallenberg Committee of Long Island

By: Brian J. Sauer"

I also wrote, and asked for a copy of the speech. There was no response to either of us.

After the Award ceremony, I sent copies of the Legislation introduced by Congressman Lent, and a copy of the letter from Senator Pell asking the Soviets to include an

American in the investigation, to the Swedish Consul General. I lost the support of Congressman Ackerman, Senator Pell, and Congressman Lent.

Senator Pell cancelled an appointment the night before I was planning to drive to Washington, and he did not reschedule. Congressman Lent discontinued work on his Resolution. Nassau County District Attorney Denis Dillon offered to speak to the Swedes to find out what they were saying that makes everyone stop being involved.

Congressman Ackerman was not mentioned in anything I gave to the Swedish Consul General. However, he could easily be found on the House Foreign Affairs Committee through Congressman Lantos, who was also a member. Arthur Flug, Congressman Ackerman's staffer, informed me that the 'family' approached Gary, and asked him not to do anything about this issue.

I wrote to Assemblyman Tom DiNapoli on November 22, 1991

"Dear Tom,

Thank you for your kind letter suggesting contacting Senator Pell. I lost him two days before your letter arrived.

I met the Swedish Consul General in New York last month. He gave an inflammatory speech saying the Soviets were lying. I asked him for a copy of the speech. (There is no official Swedish policy on Raoul Wallenberg). I gave him copies of the legislation relating to the release of the prison records and the impartial investigation. Unfortunately I also included a copy of Senator Pell's letter to the Soviets asking that an American be included in the investigation. He lost the speech within minutes, and within days Senator Pell was no longer co-operating with me.

The Demonstration in mid-October was successful in that Denis Dillon offered his support. I met with him and he suggested that this be handled just between the US and USSR if possible. It was the US that sent Mr. Wallenberg to Hungary and the US should have the responsibility of determining what happened to him. Denis offered to find out what the Swedes are saying to everyone that makes them stop being involved in this issue.

I also met with John Matthews. John did not offer to speak to Senator Pell, but offered to resurrect Mrazek and Moynihan and help with Senator D'Amato.

Maybe someday this issue will be resolved. You will have played an important role in all this with your early legislation and continued support. I am planning a Conference for all organizations worldwide who are interested in Raoul Wallenberg. It will be held the first week of August in Long Island. We would all be honored if you would address this gathering at some point.

Thank you again for everything.

Sincerely, Sharon"

To Senator Pell, I wrote:

"Dear Senator Pell:

Thank you for your letter of October 10, 1991. As you now know, it is the Swedes and not the Soviets who are opposed to learning the truth about Raoul Wallenberg's disappearance.

The U.S. has a responsibility to Raoul Wallenberg regardless of the desires of the Swedish relatives. I realize now that they have the backing of the Swedish government. They are easily able to win support in Washington. What are they gaining by refusing to resolve this issue?

Judging from the reaction of the previously supportive Congressmen and Senators who have been contacted by the

Swedish relatives, I can only assume that they are involved in some form of character assignation against me. Please give me the opportunity to defend myself!

It is my hope that reason will be focused on this Swedish plan and its merits measured by the yardstick of honesty, and failing to measure up, it forfeit its American support.

Benign neglect may be appropriate in some cases, but I think you will agree, the world is entitled to know the real truth about the disappearance of Raoul Wallenberg. It is for that reason I shall continue to struggle against powerful opposition. I may have lost support in Washington, but I still have Glen Cove!

Glen Cove made international news several years ago by refusing to allow the Soviet diplomats on the beach. The Soviets are extremely sensitive about their beautiful estate on the coastline of Long Island Sound.

Sea Cliff, where I live, is an enclave of Glen Cove. I am sure something can be worked out to move this issue further regardless of Swedish opposition.

You have made many important contributions to the quest for learning the truth about Raoul Wallenberg. I am honored to have worked with you, and will miss your support. Thank you.

Sincerely, Sharon L. Wallenberg"

Eventually, Spring came to Long Island again, and with it came the crocuses through the snow, then the daffodils, tulips, and lilacs. Hope was born again, and life continued.

Chapter Thirty-Seven: Nothing Says "Yes" Like Lilacs

Efforts to finally resolve the mystery of Raoul Wallenberg's disappearance continued. I tried to get Congressman Lent to go forward with his Resolution. Congressman Lent would not respond to me due to whatever he was told by the Swedish Government or Swedish relatives. I had to come up with another idea.

Baldwin, New York, on the South Shore of Long Island, which Congressman Norman Lent represents, is a place I visit fairly frequently. Right off the Southern State Parkway, on Grand Avenue, there is a large billboard. During election season, there is always a sign asking residents to re-elect Congressman Norman Lent. When I drove past that billboard, I wondered, "Who pays for that sign?"

I was pretty sure it was Joe Mondello, Chairman of the Nassau County Republican Party, who pays for that sign. I made an appointment with Mr. Mondello. It is common knowledge that gifts to elected officials are not allowed. This is a real blessing for low budget operations such as mine.

The morning of my appointment with Mr. Mondello, I went into my backyard and picked lilacs. I also picked parrot tulips from elsewhere in the neighborhood.

You have no idea how delighted all the employees in the Nassau County Republican Headquarters were to see those lilacs and tulips! They were a big hit with Mr. Mondello also. Ultimately, those free lilacs from the backyard turned the situation around.

I expressed my gratitude to Chairman Mondello:

"Thank you very much for your intervention with Mr. Lent. It turned things around completely and we are communicating now. I appreciate your interest and support on this important issue.

The attached letter is from the Soviet government to Glen Cove Mayor Donald De Riggi regarding an impartial investigation conducted in the Soviet Union last fall. This investigation was precipitated by Senator Moynihan's legislation which passed the full Senate last July and was presented to a Soviet official by me at an event I had in Eisenhower Park last August. Marge Rosen represented you at the event.

As you can see at the end of the letter, the evidence was taken to Sweden to become the personal possession of a few people who will not release or publish the material. The Swedish government calls the investigation unofficial and the Soviet government did not keep a record.

In order to avoid this happening again, I made the suggestion to Mr. Lent that the resolution include a provision for a delegation of US Congressmen be included in the investigation. This idea came from Assemblyman Thomas P. DiNapoli, who was the first person to ever introduce legislation for me.

If you also agree that this should be part of the Resolution in order to resolve this issue once and for all, could you please let Mr. Lent know how you feel. I am sure that he will appreciate hearing from you. Important decisions are always easier to make with lots of support and encouragement. Thank you very much.

Please enjoy the flowers I brought you from Sea Cliff. I hope they will last. The tulips looked so beautiful, but are already beginning to lose their petals. Thank you so much for everything!"

Chairman Joseph Mondello's response was:

"I am very pleased, by the way, that Norman Lent is cooperating with you and that things seem to be going in the right direction. I have taken the liberty of forwarding a copy of your most recent correspondence to Congressman Lent so that he might consider your suggestion involving the creation of a congressional delegation to participate in the investigation. Hopefully, he will consider the idea."

There was something else I learned besides nothing says 'Yes' like lilacs. That is, no matter how you influence someone to do what you want, it will never work in the long run if their heart is not in it. Conversely, it is amazing what someone can accomplish when his or her heart is in it.

Chapter Thirty-Eight: Norma's Second Conference

Norma Anderson founded the Raoul Wallenberg Committee of Jamestown, New York. I first met Norma at a black tie dinner at the Waldorf Astoria in the mid 1980's. Norma and I were seated at the same table. That was the same evening that Rabbi Frederick Werbell introduced me to Elie Wiesel.

Norma and I kept in touch, and when she asked for my assistance in getting her Wallenberg Committee going, I helped. I arranged for author Eleanor Lester, and survivor Susan Tabor, to give presentations at one of Norma's earlier meetings. At a later meeting, I interviewed Tibor Baransky, World War II Representative of the Papal Nuncio in Budapest, who was then living in Buffalo, which is near Jamestown.

Norma tried to hold a Conference on Raoul Wallenberg in Washington D.C. in the mid 1980's. Sonja Sonenfeld, of the Stockholm Wallenberg Committee, called Norma. Sonja asked if the Stockholm Wallenberg Committee could take it over and run it. Norma refused. Sonja convinced Norma to cancel it. The reason given was that it would be harmful to Wallenberg. Sonja did not say why or how.

Norma decided to try again to hold a Conference in the summer of 1991. She wanted to hold it in Long Island with my help. I suggested we include other local Wallenberg Committees – Agnes Adachi from Queens, and Leona Feldman from Philadelphia. I did all the research on accommodations, specifically dorm rooms at C.W. Post, Long Island University, transportation to and from the airport, meals, a banquet, and speakers.

The Wallenberg Committee in Manhattan held an annual meeting in a building on Park

Avenue. Norma planned to come down from Jamestown, and stay with me. We planned to attend the meeting in Manhattan together.

The Raoul Wallenberg Committee of the United States in Manhattan asked me not to attend because there was no room for me. I am 5'2", and there was not enough room for me in a *building* on Park Avenue! Most organizations want to attract people, not eliminate them. It was their meeting, so I did not attend.

Norma came down from Upstate. She stayed with me in my house in Sea Cliff. Norma went into Manhattan for the Annual Meeting. I stayed home. When Norma returned, she was furious with me. All she would say was, "No wonder your husband left you!" Actually, he did not leave me. I left him. Norma herself was divorced and remarried. What did that have to do with an Annual Meeting anyway?

Norma left without saying thank you for the hospitality or even good bye. I did not expect to hear from Norma again, but I did. She sent me a fund raising letter asking for a donation. I tossed it.

Chapter Thirty-Nine: Make the Results Public

In October 1991, the Raoul Wallenberg Committee of Long Island held an Honorary American Citizen Day Demonstration, again on Dosoris Lane. It was to request the results of the impartial investigation be made public.

The Swedes had made statements in the press that Wallenberg is alive. We asked to see the evidence upon which they based their claims.

The program included Agnes Adachi, who worked with Wallenberg in Budapest, Nassau County District Attorney Denis Dillon, Nassau County Democratic Chairman John Matthews, a Representative of County Executive Thomas Gulotta, members of the Raoul Wallenberg Committee of Long Island, Sharon Wallenberg, Brian Sauer, Barbara Bixby,

Arthur Abrams, Carol Shapiro-Siegel, Jeffrey Siegel, and for the Wallenberg statue project, sculptor George Gach and Fund Raiser Marie Sisko. Letters were read from Nassau County Republican Chairman Joseph Mondello, Congressman Mrazek, and Senator Moynihan.

The Opening remarks given by Sharon Wallenberg for Raoul Wallenberg Honorary American Citizen Day on October 12, 1991 (Christopher Columbus Day) were as follows:

"We are gathered here today on behalf of Raoul Wallenberg who, by an Act of Congress was made an Honorary American Citizen on October 5, 1981 – ten years ago this month.

Today is also Christopher Columbus Day and it is fitting that both these noble Europeans should be honored together. Both ventured out into the unknown and faced dangers – virtually alone – on a constant round the clock basis – for the sake of something they believed in. Christopher Columbus' mission was so unpopular that it was necessary to release criminals from jail to be his crew. During the journey it was necessary for Columbus to remain awake and on guard against the constant threat of mutiny by these criminals. Raoul Wallenberg also worked around the clock on his mission of saving lives. He slept very little and always in a different place to avoid the danger of the Nazis.

Both of these Europeans have significantly affected the history of the United States!

It was the American War Refugee Board, established by President Franklin Roosevelt and funded with American tax payer dollars, that Raoul Wallenberg represented on his mission of rescue. He is credited with saving 100,000 lives at great personal risk in Budapest.

At the close of World War II, Mr. Wallenberg was taken into protective custody in the Soviet Union on January 17, 1945 along with the other diplomats in Budapest. All were released except Mr. Wallenberg. The Soviets maintain that he died in prison from a heart attack in July 1947.

As a result of Demonstrations held here in Glen Cove since 1988, Legislation was introduced in New York State by Assemblyman Thomas P. DiNapoli. This was also introduced at my request in the House by Congressman Robert Mrazek and in the Senate by Senator Daniel Moynihan in 1989. The legislation asked for the release of Raoul Wallenberg's prison records. These were released by the Soviet Union in October 1989. The Moynihan Resolution was amended at my request to ask for an impartial investigation and passed the full Senate in July 1990. The investigation started that Fall.

Glen Cove Mayor, Donald DeRiggi has written to the Soviets to request the results of that investigation. In their reply they stated that there was no report.

Congressman Norman Lent had introduced Legislation at my request in January 1991 in the 102nd Congress and a new investigation is beginning. We now ask for the results of these investigations to be made public. The Swedes have made statements in the press that Wallenberg is alive and we now ask to see the evidence upon which they base that claim."

It was a beautiful fall day, and we were finally getting closer to the end.

Chapter Forty:
Senator D'Amato Confronts
the Swedes

Nassau County District Attorney Denis Dillon took the lead at this point. First he suggested that I ask Senator Alfonse D'Amato to introduce a legislative resolution which would determine what happened to Raoul Wallenberg.

Senator D'Amato agreed on December 3, 1991:

"Dear Ms. Wallenberg:

Thank you for your kind letter concerning Raoul Wallenberg and the need to continue to search for information about him.

I would be pleased to introduce a Senate Resolution requesting information about Mr. Wallenberg. In this new era, his disappearance must be solved and information about him must now be disclosed.

Please rest assured that when we come back into session in January, I will seek this resolution. I will stay in touch with you on this matter. Until then, thank you.

Sincerely, Alfonse M. D'Amato, United States Senator"

Senator Alfonse D'Amato graciously agreed to meet with Denis Dillon and me. The meeting was at his New York office near Penn Station on December 12, 1991. Denis and I drove in together.

Senator D'Amato had seemed larger than life to me. In person he looked average. However, he did what no one else so far had done. He directly confronted the Swedes regarding their claims that Raoul Wallenberg was alive in prison.

At first an aide looked shocked when I expressed concern about ending the sensationalism. I quickly added "If he is alive – *get him out*, if not – end the sensationalism." The aide looked satisfied.

Not only did Senator D'Amato confront the Swedes, he had also introduced legislation to end this seemingly endless saga. Senator Moynihan had been devoted to this issue for years, and worked very diligently on it. However, he never had the disposition or tenacity of Senator D'Amato, who was not reluctant to face the issue head on.

Before leaving our meeting, I told Senator D'Amato that when I first met the Soviet officials at their Mission in New York with Assemblyman Tom DiNapoli, they kept calling him Senator, apparently thinking he was you. Senator D'Amato said the same thing as Tom, "One Italian is the same as another."

On January 10, 1992, Senator D'Amato wrote the following letter:

"H.E. Anders Ingemar Thunborg
Embassy of Sweden, Washington D.C.

Dear Ambassador Thunborg:

I am writing to seek a clarification of the official Swedish government position on the fate of Raoul Wallenberg.

It has been brought to my attention that there appears to be a certain inconsistency in statements by Swedish officials concerning Mr. Wallenberg. Some government representatives seem to have flatly accused the Soviets of lying about his death, while others give every indication of having accepted the explanation that Wallenberg died in prison. What is the official Swedish government position on Raoul Wallenberg?

I would appreciate your help in resolving the confusion over this issue that has long been of deep interest to both our nations.

Sincerely, Alfonse M. D'Amato, United States Senator"

The Government of Sweden responded to a United States Senator a cryptic message which we interpreted to mean – Raoul Wallenberg being 'alive' is good for Swedish business. They included a brochure.

Senator D'Amato issued a press release saying the Swedes were lying. It was dated January 23, 1992 and said:

"D'AMATO SEEKS END TO WALLENBERG MYSTERY

Senator: 'Angel of Life' Merits Truthful Accounting"

Citing an outrageous 44-year span of conflicting reports concerning the alleged survival or demise of famed Holocaust hero and Swedish diplomat Raoul Wallenberg, who saved tens of thousands of Hungarian Jews in World War II, U.S. Senator Alfonse

M. D'Amato (R-NY) today introduced a Sense of the Senate Resolution calling upon President George Bush to pursue a conclusive investigation by the Russian Federation in the former Soviet Union.

Additionally, the Senator, in a January 10, 1992 letter to Swedish Ambassador Anders Thunborg, requested that the Swedish government also clarify its position on the fate of Wallenberg.

"The entire world stood silent while six million Jews were murdered in the Holocaust," said D'Amato. "While the 'Angel of Death' Joseph Mengele, sent thousands to their deaths in the gas chambers of Auschwitz, there was an 'Angel of Life' named Raoul Wallenberg, who single-handedly saved tens of thousands of Hungarian Jews."

D'Amato was joined in original cosponsorship of his resolution, which also requested that the results of the investigation be made public, by Senators Daniel Patrick Moynihan (D-NY), Joseph Lieberman (D-CT), Arlen Specter (R-PA) and William S. Cohen (R-ME).

"It is disgraceful that such a great man should be the subject of a circus atmosphere for over four decades," said D'Amato. "I don't believe we've been told the truth about Wallenberg by either the former Soviet or Swedish governments. Surely a man who has been such a towering example for humanity deserves better".

Wallenberg saved Jews in Hungary through the issuance of Swedish passports. At the end of World War II, Soviet authorities, including an officer named Leonid Brezhnev (who later in life became the Soviet President), arrested him as a suspected spy. The Soviets maintain that he died in Moscow's Lubyanka Prison in 1947.

"There were few heroes in the dark days of the Nazi Holocaust, and Raoul

Wallenberg was the greatest of them all," said the Senator. "The conquering Red Army was incapable of believing that a gentile would risk his life only to save his fellow man – in this case, the doomed Jews of Hungary.

"Common decency demands that if Wallenberg is alive, that we be blessed to see him again as a free man. If he is dead, his soul should be permitted to rest in peace. That will only happen when we learn his actual fate," concluded D'Amato."

On January 31, 1992, I wrote to Russian Deputy Valentin Lozinisky, one of my "buddies" from all the Demonstrations and Events I held, and he attended:

"Dear Valentin:

Your picture appeared on the front page of Newsday a few months ago. I was very pleased to know you and to have had you as a guest in my house. I hope everything is going well for you.

Senator Alphonse D'Amato has become involved in resolving the mystery of Raoul Wallenberg's disappearance. It is his goal to end the stalemate between the Soviet/Russian and Swedish position. It is not his goal to create animosity. I think when he questions the Soviet/Russian version he is referring to the exact nature of Mr. Wallenberg's death in a Stalinist prison.

It is my hope that something positive for the future can be created after this mystery is finally resolved. Mr. Bykov had once suggested a joint US-USSR Peace Initiative named on behalf of Mr. Wallenberg. It would be appropriate for Mr. Wallenberg's heroism, courage and humanitarianism to be continued on an international level.

Best wishes for peace and prosperity in Russia and all the other former Soviet Republics!

Sincerely, Sharon"

For the first time since the Russian Diplomats had stopped their dialogue with me, I had a response from Russian federation Diplomat, Valentin Lozinskiy on February 4, 1992

"Dear Sharon,

Thank you for your letter of January 31. I recall with much pleasure the meetings in your house and at other places. I sympathize with your continuous efforts to resolve the mystery around the fate of Raoul Wallenberg – an outstanding humanitarian activist, a real hero who fell victim of dark forces of totalitarism. I hope more could be found in the archives. Your activities to commemorate his name are highly praised and have our support. They contribute to understanding between people which is so badly needed now.

Sincerely, Valentin V. Lozinskiy"

What was in that brochure the Swedish government sent to Senator D'Amato? It informed the public that Mr. Wallenberg is presently spending his life in prison. It mentions that this issue became popular in the 1980's. Amazingly that is when Tom Lantos began to campaign for Congress. He used this issue to enhance his political appeal. He also led the Swedish relatives to ask Congressman Mrazek and Senator Moynihan, who were working to get Wallenberg's prison records released, to stop.

The pamphlet referred to a U.S. organization, The Raoul Wallenberg Committee of the United States in Manhattan. This organization was then worth about a half or three quarters of a million dollars. Their specialties included funding shenanigans and assorted sabotages of other Wallenberg projects such as a worldwide conference planned by an upstate New York Wallenberg Committee, stopping the foundry in Long Island from participating in the Long Island Wallenberg statue project, and hiring lawyers on both coasts trying to prevent the Richard Chamberlain TV movie from becoming made. They gave a cash award to Ross Perot, who certainly did not need the money. They also made sure the Conservative Rabbinical Association never gave Rabbi Werbell a congregation again.

Chapter Forty-One:
Denis Suggests McGrath

In early 1992, Nassau County District Attorney Denis Dillon suggested that Congressman Ray McGrath introduce the House Companion Resolution to Senator D'Amato's Senate Resolution.

Congressman McGrath met with me in his Long Island office in February. In March, he introduced the Resolution, House Resolution 388 in the 102nd Congress. Then he lost all interest. He never circulated a 'Dear Colleague', letter which is a required preliminary step. Further, he never returned any of Denis Dillon's phone calls. We suspected Tom Lantos' involvement.

I contacted my Congressman, Bob Mrazek, and Congressman Tom Manton to ask them to take over and circulate the 'Dear Colleague' letter. Eventually, we notified Senator D'Amato of the problem. He recruited Congressman Ben Gilman from Westchester. I met with him in Washington. That did not go very far. Again, I contacted Joe Mondello, and amazingly Congressman McGrath was resurrected in the summer, and by August, House Resolution 388 had 20 cosponsors.

By the fall of 1992, I had a new Congressman. It was someone we knew, former Nassau County Comptroller Peter King. I got him up to speed on what was going on.

Chapter Forty-Two:
The Pursuit Of Truth
Is A Noble Calling

In January 1992, I was back in the Demonstration business again. We held a Candle Light Vigil across from the Soviet Mission on Dosoris Lane in Glen Cove. This was the last Candle Light Vigil, held in the same place as the first one in 1988. This time, we asked for an end to all the sensationalism. It was expressed that the Soviet government had co-operated. It was now the responsibility of the United States government, who initiated Raoul Wallenberg's mission, to end the sensationalism.

Senator Alfonse D'Amato wrote a letter dated January 15, 1992, which included **"The pursuit of truth is a noble calling".**

"My Dear Friends:

I am pleased to greet all of you as you gather for the commemoration on the 47th anniversary of the abduction of Raoul Wallenberg.

During the time of the Holocaust, the world stood silently by as the Jews of Europe were murdered. But Raoul Wallenberg was singularly responsible for the rescue of many thousands of Hungarian Jews. He stood tall in the face of evil and darkness. It is because he existed in a world so devoid of moral precepts that no one could believe – certainly not Soviet authorities – that he was acting out of profound and unprecedented humanity.

It is for this reason that he must not be forgotten. It is for this reason that we must work together tirelessly until his true fate is ascertained with verifiable evidence. It is the very least that we can do for a man who, to this day, exemplifies the positive potential of a single individual to do so much good.

The pursuit of truth is a noble calling. I join with all of you in recalling and honoring Raoul Wallenberg.

Sincerely, Alfonse M. D'Amato, United States Senator"

In the end, that's all this really was, a noble pursuit of the truth.

Chapter Forty-Three: The Last Hurrah and Conclusion

The Last Hurrah!

The United States Resolutions and New York State Resolutions were ultimately abandoned. The strongest supporter in New York State, Assemblyman Thomas P. DiNapoli, refused to help further because he felt this was better done on the Federal level. He was probably justified in this decision.

With interest fading, and opposition constant, I was concerned that the Federal legislation would die in Committee. Judging by how difficult it had been to get support, and how quickly it always evaporated in Washington, this was probably an accurate decision.

The last event held for Raoul Wallenberg was an 80th Birthday celebration on August

4, 1992. It was at Nassau County's Chelsea Center with the Long Island Composers Alliance.

Conclusion.

After several extensive searches, no evidence to support the claim that Raoul Wallenberg survived in Soviet prison after 1947 emerged. What really happened?

The Soviet Union / Russian Federation

The Russians took Raoul Wallenberg into 'Protective Custody' on January 17, 1945. Joseph Stalin ordered all that Diplomats be taken into 'Protective Custody'. It was never a question of why Wallenberg was taken. It was always a question of why he didn't return. In the late 40's and early 50's, Diplomats returned to their countries of origin. Maj Von Dardle met the ships coming into Stockholm with the returning Diplomats. Raoul was never with them. Why? It was most likely because he was deceased.

What really happened to Raoul Wallenberg in the Russian prison? It is impossible to know this with certainty. Did Wallenberg perish as a result of harsh prison conditions? Was his death an accident or an execution? We will probably never know. If it were an execution, there are several possible explanations. First, he could have been seen as a member of one of Europe's wealthiest families. Therefore, he was an 'enemy' of Communism. Another possibility is that he was seen as a 'spy' because he was recruited by Iver Olsen, from the OSS. The OSS was a precursor to the CIA. Stalin was allegedly very paranoid about these things.

Stalin's Russia was a very brutal place. One of my colleagues from the United Nations was Russian. She was an only child, as was her Mother. One evening while watching TV in New York with her Russian born – American citizen husband, she discovered what Stalin had done to many Russians. She called her Mother in Saint Petersburg (formerly Leningrad). She found out that her Mother had many sisters and brothers who perished due to Stalin. Only her Mother survived from a large Russian family. My colleague would have had many aunts, uncles, and cousins. As a result of Stalin, she had none.

In any event, it is unlikely that we will ever know any more than we do now about Raoul Wallenberg's disappearance. What we do know is that there is no evidence to support the claim that Raoul Wallenberg survived in Soviet prison after 1947.

Raoul Wallenberg was not a representative of animosity, but of compassion. I do not think he would want to be remembered as a reason for hate, but rather for forgiveness and love. It is no tribute to Raoul Wallenberg's memory to use him as a vehicle for ill will. To their credit, Gorbachev's Russia went above and beyond reasonable expectations in trying to resolve this mystery, and honor Raoul Wallenberg.

The Swedish Government

Sweden is a relatively defenseless nation with a neighbor which is historically one of the most aggressive nations on earth. The Swedes' only defense is NATO. They have little control over that. Perhaps, after living for generations in these circumstances any opportunity to retaliate becomes blurred in respect to the veracity of the claim. We will never know. Senator Alfonse D'Amato said the Swedes were lying. We also took their position to be that Raoul Wallenberg being "alive" is good for Swedish business. In any event, their claims were not valid.

The Swedish Relatives

Senator Pell suggested that the relatives were distraught. It is understandable that the disappearance of a family member could cause this. Circumstances suggest that the relatives and their friends may have been receiving some kind of benefit from claiming that Raoul Wallenberg was 'alive'.

It is interesting that Betty Throne-Holst, Nina Lagergren's friend and neighbor for nearly twenty years in Stockholm, said in a recorded interview with Frederick Werbell, that Mrs. Lagergren had never mentioned the name of Raoul Wallenberg. Mr. Werbell's book was published in Sweden without an author's name on it. This is extremely unusual, and perhaps unheard of. I saw the book. It is true. This shows the extent of the influence of those who disagree with the facts. In addition, Mrs. Lagergren's husband was conspicuously absent in all activities regarding Raoul Wallenberg. Anyone who spoke to the relatives and their friends got the impression that they were lying. We will never know for certain what their motivation was. However, considering that they are Raoul Wallenberg's relatives, it is preferable to just assume that they were "distraught".

Congressman Tom Lantos

Why did Congressman Tom Lantos stop any efforts to discover the whereabouts of Raoul Wallenberg? Why didn't Lantos do anything to help Raoul Wallenberg during his first ten years in Congress? Again, we will probably never know for sure. However, according to sources in California, Mr. Lantos exploited many issues, not just this one, for his own benefit. How did he benefit from preventing the Raoul Wallenberg issue from being resolved? That is unclear. What is clear is that he was behind all attempts in Washington to destroy the resolution of this issue. We will probably never know why.

The Raoul Wallenberg Committee of the United States

The Raoul Wallenberg Committee of the United States in Manhattan had a mandate to 'inform and inspire'. This did not include finding out what happened to Raoul Wallenberg. They maintained that he was alive, but did not participate in attempts to secure his release. They did however, considerably profit financially when the prison records were released. None of this money was shared with those on a shoestring budget actually doing the work, and incurring the expenses. The Raoul Wallenberg Committee of the United States turned into a lucrative business without any substantial results. They jealously guarded their position by discrediting, or trying to discredit others. They persuaded the Conservative Rabbinical Organization not to allow Rabbi Frederick Werbel to have a congregation again. Werbel's article in the New York Times Magazine started all the interest in Raoul Wallenberg. They would not allow me to be on their mailing list until I mailed them a copy of my birth certificate, marriage certificate, and divorce decree. They prevented a statue of Raoul Wallenberg from being built in Long Island by persuading donors not to get involved.

This may not be the story you were expecting, but it is what I promised in the beginning: **The Truth.**

Sharon Wallenberg and Joel Meisner, of
Meisner Foundry, going to an 'Evening of
Magic' at the Waldorf Astoria honoring Alan
Greenberg of the Raoul Wallenberg
Committee of the United States, Manhattan.
May 1, 1991.

328

Last Demonstration in Glen Cove
Requesting the Results of the Impartial
Investigation be made public. Nassau
County District Attorney Denis Dillon, then
Glen Cove Mayor Thomas Suozzi, the
Soviet compound. October 12, 1991.

330

Sharon Wallenberg receives a Proclamation from County Executive Thomas Gulotta Representative August 1992.

Part Three

Going

Forward

Chapter Forty-Four: Lessons Learned

Going forward, possibly the greatest tribute we can give to our beloved hero, Raoul Wallenberg, is to learn the lessons he taught us, and carry them forward in today's world. If there is anything we learned from Raoul Wallenberg, and his selfless sacrifice, it is the qualities of compassion, determination, and imagination. One person can make a difference!

The most important thing now is to emulate these qualities in our own lives. If you admire someone, you want to be like that person. After all, imitation is the sincerest form of flattery!

Going forward, we need to apply lessons learned of Wallenberg's quality of compassion to all aspects of existence. That is, to other people, other sentient beings, and our planet.

Chapter Forty-Five: War and Its Aftermath

The history of warfare goes all the way back to Cain and Abel.

Today's concern is "terror". I was in Manhattan at a UN event the evening before September 11, 2001. I was inside the New York City limits that morning. One of my best friends, Yolanda Dowling, perished in the World Trade Center. I lived through that, and like everyone else, experienced emotions. The thing I wanted most during that time of death was for no one else to die – not even those responsible. I wanted them punished, but not killed.

There was so much death in the following weeks! I was lucky enough to be able to leave all the death, fire, and smoke behind, and go to Florida. I was still crying in Florida. I looked at the ocean waves, and saw the towers falling down over, and over again.

Martin Luther King once said, "Violence is the language of the unheard". While greed, plunder, and financial gain can cause violence, this is unfortunately one of the causes of terror. In other words, what is our part in causing this? Are we following Raoul Wallenberg's example of selfless compassion?

Currently the U.S. is facilitating a brutal bombing campaign in Yemen. So far, over 3,800 civilians, including women and children, have been killed by the U.S. backed coalition. The coalition has committed war crimes, violated international humanitarian law, and allowed ISIS and Al Qaeda to expand their territory in Yemen. In one case, a U.S. drone targeted a convoy of vehicles – a bridegroom and his family going to his wedding. They were all killed before arriving at the bride's home for the wedding.

This unnecessary destruction of life and property is in no way a reflection of Raoul Wallenberg's compassion. In fact, Raoul Wallenberg was on his way to meet with the Russians to discuss his plans for reconstruction when he was taken into "protective custody". As an architect, he believed in building, not destroying.

Wars of aggression by renegade regimes are better handled by the United Nations Peacekeepers. The United States is not the world's policeman. Funds, troops, and weapons to combat legitimate acts of aggression should be given to the United Nations for peace keeping operations. They are as capable of success as any other army. This would also deflect acts of retaliation away from any one country.

National military forces should be used with the restraint of unarmed Wallenberg. Vera Stern, a Budapest survivor, told me she saw Wallenberg telling an elderly Jewish man to go inside a Swedish Safe House. Vera thought he was harsh, but minutes later several Nazis armed with machine guns came along, and began to harass the man. Unarmed, Wallenberg grabbed the Nazis by the lapels and shook them. Courage trumps blind aggression any day.

For More Information: Peace Action

Chapter Forty Six:
Our Fellow Travelers

Our fellow travelers on "Spaceship Earth", or as Buddha calls them, "sentient beings", deserve nothing less from us than the compassion personified by Raoul Wallenberg.

Compassionate Israelis of all ages, both men and women, are tattooing the number 269 on their forearms. This is reminiscent of World War II concentration camp practices of tattooing prisoner numbers on forearms. The prisoner in this case is 269, a white Israeli calf. He was rescued or stolen, from a slaughterhouse by saviors, or terrorists, depending on your point of view.

The immensely popular 269 movement in Israel is indicative of a worldwide movement towards kinder, more compassionate treatment of our fellow travelers on spaceship earth. In short, there is a worldwide movement towards compassion by many people who have never even heard of Raoul Wallenberg.

What we eat shows our compassion. Each year more than 5 billion pigs, cows, calves, turkeys, and fish are killed in the United States for food. On factory farms where most meat, dairy, and eggs come from, animals are crammed into cages so small that they cannot even turn around. Babies are taken from mothers, often as soon as they are born. Male chicks in egg facilities are ground up alive. Disease is so prevalent in these conditions that antibiotics are routinely fed to animals causing antibiotic resistance in humans.

Poultry. More chickens are farmed than any other animal. Over nine billion chickens are produced, and slaughtered each year. The scale of their suffering is unimaginable. Tens of thousands of chickens are kept in sheds where there is no natural light. The air is unbreathable due to ammonia from urine. Baby chicks have their beaks and toes cut off to prevent fighting due to extreme overcrowding. Debeaking cuts through bone, cartilage, and soft tissue without benefit of pain relief. Chickens raised for meat are genetically altered to grow twice as fast, and twice as large, as normal chickens. This causes multiple health issues for these birds. Unhealthy living conditions expose the chickens to all kinds of disease.

Transportation to slaughter is done by the cheapest means possible. The chickens are packed in crates on the backs of trucks unprotected from weather conditions. Birds literally freeze to death in winter, or die from heat stress, and suffocation in summer. At the slaughterhouse, crates of chickens are removed from trucks with cranes or forklifts, and dumped on a conveyor belt. As birds are unloaded, some fall on the floor where they die from being crushed by machinery or vehicles, or they die slowly from starvation, and neglect. Fully conscious birds are hung by their feet on a moving rail. Stunning is not required because chickens and poultry are not covered by the Humane Slaughter Act. They are killed as cheaply as possible, regardless of the additional suffering it causes. The birds' throats are slashed, usually by a mechanical blade which often misses. Then the dead, and the live chickens, are submerged in boiling water. Birds missed by the killing blade are boiled alive. This is such a common occurrence that these birds are called 'redskins'. Don't eat chickens.

Eggs are produced by huge agribusiness corporations. Hens are kept in crowded battery cages where their most basic instincts are cruelly violated. There is no natural light. Four or five hens are in each cage. They cannot walk, or stretch their wings. Their feathers fall out, their skin becomes raw, and often bloody, and their feet are injured, and often caught, by the wire floor. When the hen's feet become caught in the wire floor, it can prevent her from reaching food. Hens can slowly starve to death inches from food. Dead hens remain in the cage with living hens.

To prevent cannibalism, hens are debeaked. A hot blade cuts through bone, cartilage, and soft tissue. Many birds die from shock during the process. The industry uses enormous amounts of antibiotics, pesticides, and other chemicals. Pesticides are fed to the hens so that their excrement attracts fewer flies. Eggs yolks are chemically dyed to achieve a yellow look, which in nature comes from the sun.

When egg production falls off, the industry starves, and denies hens water, for several days. This 'forced molting' shocks the hens into losing whatever feathers they have left, and starts a new egg laying cycle. Many hens die during this tortuous cycle. There is no veterinary care. Dying hens are thrown on 'dead piles' with the dead hens.

Male chicks are of no use to the egg industry. Newborn baby male chicks are thrown into plastic garbage bags. They suffocate slowly under the weight of the other chicks dumped on top of them. Male chicks are also ground up for animal feed while still alive. Don't eat eggs, or anything made with eggs.

Turkeys are slaughtered at the rate of about 300 million a year. Most turkeys are raised in confinement. Disease and suffering are rampant in these inhumane conditions. Stressed turkeys are driven to fighting, causing 'economic' loss. To prevent 'loss', the turkey's beaks and toes are cut off without pain relief. Turkeys have been anatomically manipulated to grow abnormally fast and large. If a seven pound baby grew at the same rate as the turkeys are forced to, the baby would weigh 1500 pounds at 18 weeks of age. When turkeys reach market weight, they are packed in crates, and shipped to slaughter. Fully conscious turkeys are hung upside down by metal shackles. They suffer from pain, and terror, as they are carried on a conveyor belt. Then they have their throats cut. They are not stunned, and as a result, turkeys are bled to death while fully conscious. The killing methods are not precise, so many turkeys go into tanks of boiling water while still alive. Don't eat turkeys.

Foie Gras is produced from ducks and geese who are a few months old. These unfortunate birds are confined in dark sheds, and force fed large amounts of food several times a day. A worker grabs the bird, and forces a metal pipe down its neck. Then a mechanized pump shoots a mixture of corn and oil directly into their gullets. This is done for a few weeks, during which time many birds die from ruptured, punctured throats, burst stomachs, and other ailments. They are dehydrated because they are not given sufficient amounts of water. In addition, they are often debeaked to prevent stressed birds from injuring each other in crowded conditions. Debeaking is done by a hot blade cutting through bone, cartilage, and soft tissue without any pain relief. The birds' enlarged livers are sold as a 'gourmet' food item after a horrific slaughter. Foie gras production is banned in the United Kingdom, Austria, Czech Republic, Denmark, Finland, Sweden, Norway, Poland, Switzerland, and Israel. It should be banned in the United States also.

Beef cattle are often born, and live, on ranches unprotected from inclement weather. Thousands die because ranchers do not think it is economical to provide shelter, or veterinary care to injured, ill or otherwise ailing animals. These animals have holes punched in their ears for identification tags. These tags have numbers, not names. Cattle are branded with hot irons, which is extremely painful and traumatic. Cattle are often transported for hundreds or thousands of miles. By law, they are allowed to travel for up to 36 hours without food or water. Thousands of cattle die every year from overcrowding or stress. At stockyards and auctions, frightened animals are kicked or shocked, and sold to the highest bidder. From there they go to slaughter or a feedlot. Younger cattle spend the last few months of their lives ingesting growth hormones, and being fed an abnormal diet designed to produce fast growth. Sick and diseased livestock are common in these filthy places. Small planes flying over can smell the stench from high above the feedlots. At slaughter, conditions make it nearly impossible to treat the animals with any semblance of humanity. Although cattle are covered by the Human Slaughter Act, it is seldom enforced. Don't eat beef.

Dairy cows live short, confined lives of forced births, unnatural feeds, painful injections, and calcium depleted bones. To produce milk, dairy cows must give birth. They produce a calf a year, which is taken from them soon after birth. Mother cows mourn the loss of their baby calves.   The cows endure a physically demanding nine month gestation period, during which time they give milk for the first seven months. With genetic mutation, cows produce 100 pounds of milk a day – ten times more than in nature. Their udders are so heavy and swollen that they are in constant pain and are unable to walk properly. Hormones banned in Europe and Canada are used in the United States to increase milk production. This causes birth defects in the calves. The cows are fed unnatural diets which cause disease, some of which are fatal. All dairy cows suffer from diseases directly related to the way they are treated. In nature, cows live about 20 years, in the dairy industry, they are 'unproductive', spent, and slaughtered at about three or four years old. They are slaughtered in horrific ways, and become low grade hamburger, and low quality beef products. Don't eat or drink dairy.

"Downed cows" are worn out, depleted dairy cows who are so weak, and diseased from the lives they have been forced to live, that they cannot stand. These "downers" are still sold for human consumption. They are typically left without food, water, or care, for days until it is convenient to take them to slaughter. Usually they are moved by the most convenient, least humane ways, such as being dragged or pushed with tractors or forklifts. This causes even more suffering and injuries. Downed animals are not protected from abuse under federal animal welfare laws, no matter how cruel the treatment is.

Veal calves are the by-product of the dairy industry. Male calves are not able to produce milk, so they are taken from their mothers, chained by the neck, and kept in crates so small they cannot turn around, stretch, or lie down. Their muscles are not able to develop, keeping their meat 'tender'. They are fed a poor diet, making them anemic. These sick, abused animals produce pale-colored flesh. These inhumane conditions cause the calves to be more likely to develop diseases than cattle in more normal circumstances. Veal calves requires copious amounts of medication to keep them alive until slaughter at a few months of age. Veal is the most likely meat to contain illegal drug residues which pose a threat to human consumption. Don't eat veal.

Pork. Approximately 100 million pigs are raised and slaughtered in the United States every year. In nature, pigs live in social groups in light woodlands. They are as intelligent as dogs, naturally very clean, and are very active. Pregnant sows build large nests where they give birth, and protect their piglets. The piglets are weaned in nature from milk to solid food at 10 – 20 weeks.

In factory farms, piglets are taken from their grieving Mothers as young as three weeks old. They are housed in indoor barren, over crowded pens. There is no straw or other bedding. They lie on concrete. Each sow is forced to have 20 piglets per year. Of all pigs, the breeding sows are treated the most cruelly. They live in a continual cycle of artificial insemination from masturbated male pigs, birth, and re-impregnation. The sows are confined in small, metal gestation crates. For their entire lives, the sows cannot walk or turn around, and barely have room to stand up. They are denied straw bedding, and must lie on concrete. They mourn the loss of their babies, as any other mother would. Their physical, and psychological suffering is immense.

After piglets are taken from their mothers, their tails are cut off with pliers, or a hot docking iron, without pain relief causing permanent pain. Males are castrated without pain relief. The mutilations cause pain, illness, and even death. Approximately 15% of the piglets die soon after leaving their mothers. The surviving pigs endure horrific circumstances until their death at six months of age. After three or four years, the breeding sows are no longer deemed productive, and are sent to slaughter. Don't eat pork, ham, or bacon.

Toronto Pig Save is a Canadian organization of people who witness outside a slaughterhouse. They give the doomed pigs an act of kindness, which is probably the first, and last of their lives. Starving, thirsty pigs are given a drink of water before their horrific deaths. For this Raoul Wallenberg type of active compassion, the founder was jailed.

Humane Meat, Milk, and Eggs. All animals raised "humanely" are subjected to the same cruel transportation, handling, and slaughter methods as factory farmed animals. Poultry is not covered by the Humane Slaughter Law. All chickens are killed as cheaply as possible without any consideration for the amount of suffering it causes. 'Humane' chickens are still debeaked. Male chicks in the 'humane' egg industry are still suffocated, or ground up. 'Free range' eggs do not have any set standard. The hens may simply be in slightly larger cages, or be allowed out in barren dirt areas for brief times. Cows used for 'humane' milk are still repeatedly impregnated. Their babies are taken from them. They are forced to give milk while pregnant, and they are forced to produce more milk than they would in nature. Unwanted male calves in the 'humane' dairy industry are still sold for veal as young as a few days old. No animal, humanely raised or not, volunteers for a

351

horrific slaughter. Don't be fooled by false claims.

Fish caught in the wild are killed in the most horrific, inhumane ways. Often nets that are miles long are used. These nets catch and kill many untargeted individual fish, who are just in the wrong place, at the wrong time. There are no regulations to insure humane treatment of fish. Fish plants in the U.S. make no effort to stun fish. Fish are completely conscious when they are cut. They convulse in pain as they die.

With oceans becoming exhausted, more than 40% of all fish consumed each year are now raised on aqua farms. These fish spend their entire lives in cramped, filthy enclosures. They suffer from parasites, diseases, and injuries. The United Nations Food and Agriculture Organization (UNFAO) reports that the aquaculture industry is growing three times faster than land based animal agriculture. Deformities and stress related injuries are common, and as many as 40% of the farmed fish are blind due to the horrific conditions they are raised in. Because they are designed to navigate vast oceans using all their senses, they go insane from cramped conditions, and lack of space. Salmon farms are intensely crowded with as many as 50,000 individuals in an enclosure. Don't eat fish, farmed or wild.

Lobsters carry their young for nine months, and can live 100 years. Researcher Michael Kuba says that lobsters are "amazingly smart." They establish social relationships, and take long-distance seasonal journeys of 100 miles or more each year. When kept in tanks, they suffer from the stress of confinement, low oxygen levels, and crowding. Neurobiologist Tom Abrams says that lobsters have "a full array of senses." Lobsters may feel even more pain than we would in similar situations. According to invertebrate zoologist Jaren G. Horsley, "The lobster does not have an autonomic nervous system that puts it into a state of shock when it is harmed. It probably feels itself being cut…I think the lobster is in a great deal of pain from being cut open…and feels all the pain until its nervous system is destroyed during cooking". Don't eat lobster.

Crabs have well-developed senses of sight, smell, and taste. Research indicates that they have the ability to feel pain. Dr. Robert Elwood, from Queens University in Belfast, who has studied crustaceans for decades, says "Denying that crabs feel pain because they don't have the same biology as mammals is like denying they can't see because they don't have a visual cortex." Millions of crabs are caught, and killed yearly in the United States. With these doomed crabs, are birds, fish, and other marine animals, who are thrown back into the water dead or dying. Don't eat crabs.

Shrimp is perhaps the most popular of all the shell fish. Each one is an individual who had a life and, suffered death. They did not volunteer to be someone's dinner or appetizer. They preferred to live a long and happy life with their friends and family, just like everyone else. Have a heart. Don't eat shrimp.

For more information: Farm Sanctuary

The meat, fish, and dairy based diet has been linked to Heart Disease, Cancer, Diabetes, and Erectile Dysfunction.

Heart Disease and Erectile Dysfunction occur when plaques composed of cholesterol and fat from meat, fish, and dairy form in the arteries, preventing normal blood flow. The body produces enough of its own cholesterol. Meat, fish, and dairy add extra unneeded cholesterol which ultimately restricts blood flow causing heart disease, strokes, and erectile dysfunction.

Diabetes occurs when fat from meat, fish, and dairy fills the body's cells. This makes it impossible for glucose from digestion to enter, and nourish the cells. All food -

protein, carbohydrate, and fat - is broken down by the digestive process into glucose, a simple sugar. Glucose is used to nourish all the cells of the body. If glucose cannot enter, and nourish fat filled cells, it stays in the blood stream. Glucose, simple sugar, is removed from the blood by the kidneys and is excreted in urine causing the symptoms of diabetes.

Cancer starts when something goes wrong in a cell. The cell begins multiplying out of control, and forms a tumor. Meat, fish, and dairy products are high in hormones, and other carcinogens which speed the growth of abnormal cells. Meat, fish, and dairy contain no fiber, which is necessary to eliminate excess hormones, and toxins from the body. The plant based diet is high in protein, contains antioxidants, and protective nutrients which help prevent cancer, and also contains fiber which facilitates the removal of carcinogens and toxins.

A compassionate vegan diet can prevent heart disease, cancer, diabetes, and erectile dysfunction. Try it.

For more information: Physicians Committee For Responsible Medicine (PCRM)

There are a plethora of compassionate choices available for those who care about their own health, and the well-being of our fellow travelers on spaceship Earth. There are plant milks: soy, almond and coconut; non- dairy frozen desserts, meat substitutes like meatless meatballs, chic'kn cutlets, crabless cakes, and many more. There is even delicious non-bacon. Holidays can be festive with cruelty free, and delicious tofurky. Think of Raoul Wallenberg, and his compassion, when you make culinary choices.

What we wear reflects our level of compassion. Leather, fur, down, and wool are not compassionate choices. Synthetic and faux alternatives are available. They are compassionate, practical, and attractive.

Leather is a big business. It often involves completely conscious cows, and calves, being skinned alive, or thrown into scalding hot tanks. Dog and cat skins from Asia are used without being labeled as such. Much leather comes from India where the leather trade is perhaps the cruelest in the world. Most Indian animals used for leather are so sick and injured by the time they arrive at the slaughterhouse that they must be dragged. Many have hot chili peppers, and tobacco rubbed into their eyes. Their tail bones are painfully twisted, and broken. This is to force the weak animals into the slaughterhouse. Once inside, their throats are slit. Some have their legs hacked off, or are skinned while still alive. Do not wear leather.

Fur comes from animal such as foxes, minks, rabbits and others, who live their lives in cruel confinement. Then they are anally or vaginally electrocuted, or bludgeoned to death. Do not wear fur.

Wool. Sheep are docile, gentle animals who feel pain, fear, and loneliness. If not genetically manipulated, they would grow just enough wool to protect themselves from temperature extremes. Their fleece provides insulation from cold and heat.

Shearers are paid by volume, not by the hour, which encourages them to work quickly without any regard for the welfare of the sheep. Their carelessness leads to frequent injuries. Large wounds are sewn with needle and threat, and no pain relief. Strips of skin, teats, tail, and ears are often carelessly cut off during shearing. Sheep are punched, kicked, and stomped on, and hit in the face with electric clippers while being sheared. Workers stand on the sheep's heads, necks, and hind legs. One shearer was seen hitting a lamb on the head with a hammer. Another used a sheep's body to wipe her own urine off the floor. Another shearer repeatedly twisted, and bent a sheep's neck, breaking it. In one case, a sheep died, was roasted, and eaten, by workers in full view of the other sheep, who knew what was going on.

A commonly used process called 'mulesing" involves cutting huge chunks of skin from the sheep's' backside without painkillers. Within weeks of birth, lambs' ears are hole punched, their tails chopped off, and males are castrated without painkillers. Male lambs are castrated between 2 and 8 weeks old, either by making an incision, and cutting their testicles off, or with a rubber ring used to cut off blood supply – one of the most painful methods of castration possible. If the lamb's testicles do not fall off, they are cut off with clippers. Every year, hundreds of lambs die before the age of 8 weeks from exposure or starvation. Mature sheep die every year from disease, lack of shelter, and neglect.

Unwanted Australian sheep are shipped to the Middle East on crowded multilevel ships. These voyages can last for weeks. There is no food or water available for the sheep. When they arrive, they are dragged by their ears or legs, and slaughtered while still conscious. Standards and humane laws are non-existent there. Do not wear wool.

Down involves pulling the feathers out of ducks and geese, and leaving them bleeding and suffering. Many do not survive the ordeal. Do not buy down.

Can you enjoy wearing something that has caused unspeakable suffering? Think of Raoul Wallenberg and make compassionate choices in clothing.

Entertainment involves making compassionate choices. Animals used for entertainment in circuses, rodeos, zoos, aquariums, and seaquariums lead completely unnatural lives. There is nothing compassionate about being entertained by a captive orca. Tilikum, the orca, was featured in the documentary "Blackfish". He was not alone. Lolita, another popular orca, has languished for nearly 50 years in Miami. She is in the smallest tank in North America. Orcas are social animals like elephants. Like many other orcas, Lolita has not had the companionship of family, friends, or any other orcas in nearly 50 years.

Zoos, pseudo-sanctuaries, traveling shows, and roadside displays use animals who are forced to spend their lives behind bars just to entertain the public. These animals live completely unnatural lives. Living conditions are often dismal, with animals confined to filthy, barren enclosures. Even the best environments can't come close to matching the freedom that animals want and need. Animals are bored, lonely, and often abused by their caregivers. The symptoms of their suffering are rocking, swaying, pacing endlessly, and hurting themselves. Don't go to zoos, aquariums, or sea shows.

Circuses are another cruel choice in entertainment. Animals in circuses are not volunteers. They are beaten, shocked with electric prods or small hand held easily concealed devices, chained, and whipped to make them perform unnatural and often dangerous tricks. Bullhooks, long sticks with sharp metal hooks, are used to discipline elephants. Elephants, big cats, bears, horses, and primates are beaten with sticks, axe handles, baseball bats, and metal pipes in order to break their spirits, and show them "who's boss".

Whips are used violently in training and cause lingering, intense pain. They are used again in performances as a reminder of what is waiting if the animal is unwilling or physically unable to perform correctly. In 2000 in White Plains, New York, an elephant named Petunia was beaten to death by ten trainers, for failing to perform her trick correctly due to advanced, untreated arthritis.

Most circus elephants were captured in the wild. Baby elephants born to these traumatized mothers are removed at birth, tied with ropes, and kept in isolation until they learn to fear their trainers. Then they are brutally "trained" which often leads to death. The mothers grieve inconsolably.

Tigers are naturally afraid of fire. 'Training' tigers so severely traumatizes them that they are willing to jump through hoops of fire. Tigers can become caught in these hoops, and suffer severe burns, if they survive.

Big cats, bears, primates and other animals are forced to eat, drink, sleep, defecate, and urinate in the same cramped cages. They are often transported around the country in the worst conditions. A young tiger named Clyde died from heat while being transported though the Mohave dessert. His train car was not checked by circus personnel for days.

There are many animal free circuses in the United States. Children can have fun without causing animals to suffer. Patronize cruelty free circuses, not animal circuses.

Rodeos are not compassionate. Animals used in rodeos are not aggressive by nature. Without the use of spurs, tail twisting, and bucking straps cinched tightly around their abdomen and groin, these frightened, and often docile animals wouldn't even buck. Bulls and horses are tormented in the chutes prior to being released into the ring. The animals are terrorized into action when these 'brave' cowboys and cowgirls shove electric prods into them, twist their necks, yank them by their tails or legs, slam them to the ground, and otherwise batter them.

Injuries to these animals include deep internal organ bruising, hemorrhaging, bone fractures, ripped tendons, torn ligaments and muscles. The animals are used repeatedly before finally being sent to slaughter. They arrive at slaughterhouses so extensively bruised that often the only areas in which the skin is attached to the body is the head, neck, legs and belly. Rodeo animals can have as many as six or eight broken ribs protruding from the spine, often puncturing their lungs. It is not uncommon for there to be two or three gallons of free blood accumulated under the detached skin. Inspectors in slaughterhouses say the rodeo animals are in the worst condition they have ever seen. Don't go to rodeos.

Animal racing is not like athletic racing. Horses and dogs do not decide to race the way human athletes do. Instead, first they are breed through horrific methods. Mares (female horses) are immobilized using painful devices. Then a group of ten men forces the stallion (male horse) on the mare. No matter how much the stallion refuses, he cannot escape from the ten men. Stallions are used like this hundreds of times during a breeding season for steep stud fees. The female is impregnated repeatedly in search of the perfect offspring who can win races, and enrich their owners. The colts who show promise are subjected to many brutal, often life threatening techniques, to enhance performance. The many, many horses who do not make the grade are eliminated in the most horrific ways. Do not patronize horse races. Horses don't bet on humans; humans shouldn't bet on horses.

Dogs, specifically greyhounds, used in racing are killed when they don't show promise for a racing career. Those who do race are killed when they no longer produce a profit. They are shot, bludgeoned, or euthanized. One track in Florida kills approximately 600 to 800 dogs yearly. Greyhounds are characteristically gentle and undemanding. They seldom bite no matter what pain or indignities are inflicted on them. Don't patronize dog racing.

Horse-drawn carriages are often struck by vehicles resulting in severe injuries or death to horses, drivers, passengers, and passer-bys. Horses can become frightened, and race into traffic or onto sidewalks. Often veterinary care is refused by carriage owners for horses' injuries. Horses are subjected to blistering heat and humidity, hot and hard pavement, traffic congestion, exhaust fumes, constant exposure to sun, long hours, inadequate rest, and are given little or no water. Their lives are jeopardized when they cannot cool themselves. Pavement temperature is often 50 degrees hotter than air. Horses enslaved by the carriage industry usually return from a treacherous day's work to a filthy hard floor without clean bedding, no access to pasture, and inadequate food and water. They are often malnourished. They are prevented from socializing with each other, and often tied to poles. Have compassion; don't ride in horse-drawn carriages.

I cannot imagine Raoul Wallenberg patronizing these forms of entertainment. Can you?

Animal experimental is outdated and cruel. There are models available which more closely, and accurately, represent the human body, and do not cause unnecessary and cruel suffering to animals in labs. Because of physiological variations between species, human reactions to drugs differ from those of animals.

Millions of rabbits, guinea pigs, rats and other mammals are force-fed cosmetics and household products. This results in convulsions, vomiting, and bleeding from the eyes, nose, mouth, and even death. Animals cower in fear in barren cages, often causing them to self-mutilate. Cages have been put through automatic washing machines while the animals are still in them. This carelessness scalds them to death. Dogs and cats who were formerly household pets are procured from Class B Dealers.

These former pets often still have their collars on during painful, often deadly experiments. The only interaction lab animals have with humans is when they are restrained so that painful procedures can be performed, or when they are euthanized.

Baby chimps are taken at birth from their mothers. These mothers have been constrained at the neck, wrists, waist, and ankles, immobilizing them with their legs spread apart, on the so called 'rape rack'. The female chimps are repeatedly artificially inseminated by male lab workers to cause conception. The baby chimps, and their mothers, never experience a single act of kindness during their sometimes 30 years of life. The baby chimps' grow up constantly having blood drawn, being infected with various deadly diseases, and then are categorized as DNR – do not resuscitate.

Drugs can represent cruelty. For example, Premarin is the ultimate in cruelty, and can often cause severe side effects in the women who use it. Premarin stands for PREgnant MARes urINe, or pregnant mare's urine. Mares (female horses) are artificially inseminated, and forced to stand in stalls so small that they cannot lie down, or turn around. Cups are attached to their bodies to catch their urine. Water is restricted, causing the pregnant mares to be dehydrated when their body most needs water. This unhealthy, cruel treatment produces urine which is highly concentrated with hormones. When the baby colt is born, he or she is removed, and killed as an unwanted by-product of the drug industry. The poor mare who just lost her baby is impregnated again - if she is still standing. If not, she is also killed after a life of unbearable physical and emotional misery.

The purpose of this drug is to relieve symptoms of menopause in women. It has caused physical problems in women who are taking it. Vegan women do not use premarin or hormone replacement therapy (HRT) because they do not need it. Soy mimics estrogen in women's bodies. Menopausal symptoms can be relieved by eating tofu. There are no adverse effects to men or boys from eating soy.

In addition, for relief of menopausal symptoms, there are cruelty free products such as Estriol-Care, and Natural Progesterone Cream. There are also bio-identical hormones synthetically produced in Labs from plant sources. These possess the same molecular structure as natural hormones. Dietary phytoestrogens are naturally occurring substances found in fruits, vegetables, and whole grains such as soy beans and alfalfa sprouts, and oil seeds such as flax seeds, which also reduce the intensity and frequency of hot flashes.

For more information; Physicians Committee for Responsible Medicine (PCRM)

Remember, show compassion to our fellow travelers on spaceship earth in what you eat, wear and do. Please be compassionate always like Raoul Wallenberg was. It requires courage to pursue this path, and determination not to give up when others around you do not act compassionately.

What is the point of admiring Raoul Wallenberg if we do not learn from him, and transform our lives to be compassionate, determined and imaginative like him?

Chapter Forty-Seven: Spaceship Earth

Climate Change is threatening our home, spaceship earth, in unprecedented ways. It is destroying small island nation states, and eroding coastal areas. Climate Change is directly linked to human behavior. Again, the lessons learned from Raoul Wallenberg come into play. The situation requires courage, and determination. It requires courage in making difficult decisions, and determination in implementing, and continuing to implement them.

Warmer climate is caused by carbon dioxide and methane – greenhouse gases in the atmosphere. This is caused by transportation, energy, mechanized farming, and deforestation, among other causes. Of all causes, the livestock sector generates the most greenhouse gas emissions according to a United Nations Food and Agriculture Organization (UNFAO) report.

Global warming melts polar ice caps, and mountain glaciers, causing increases in sea levels that threaten coastal areas, and small island nation. Tsunamis, hurricanes, earthquakes, droughts, and floods have been scientifically linked to CO_2 emissions.

There is a deep injustice in climate change. Rich countries grow richer, while causing the problem. The poorest countries are the most affected, and have the least responsibility for the cause. Food, water, and security issues are execrated by the droughts and floods brought on by global warming.

Meat production does more to cause global warming than any other source. The massive amount of animal feces produced in factory farms is the largest source of airborne methane in the United States. Methane traps heat in the atmosphere almost 25 times more effectively than carbon dioxide does. Animals raised for food in the United States produce 130 times more excrement than the entire human population does – 86,000 pounds per second. A typical pig factory generates a quantity of raw waste equal to that of a city of 50,000 people, but without the sewage system. The runoff from factory farms pollutes rivers and lakes more than all other industrial sources combined.

Of all agricultural land in the U.S., nearly 80% is used to raise animals for food. More than 260 million acres of U.S. forest have been cleared to create cropland to grow grain to feed farmed animals. Twenty times more land is required to feed a meat-eater than to feed a vegan. Raising animals for food consumes nearly half the water used in the U.S. It takes 2,500 gallons of water to produce a pound of beef, but only 25 gallons to produce a pound of wheat. Chicken, hog, and cattle excrement have polluted 35,000 miles of rivers in 22 states, and contaminated groundwater in 17 states.

More than one third of all the raw materials, and non-renewable fossil fuels used in the United States, are required to raise animals for food. This includes fuel to produce fertilizer for the crops that are fed to animals, oil to run the trucks that take them to slaughter, electricity to freeze their carcasses, and much more. These flesh and blood, sentient creatures are killed in ways that would horrify any compassionate person.

Unsustainable energy is another cause of Climate Change. The United Nations

Decade of Sustainable Energy For All promises to transform the global energy landscape with energy from clean, efficient, reliable, renewable energy.

The world is undergoing a shift from a fossil fuel economy to a sustainable energy economy by developing energy from renewable sources: solar, wind, hydro, biomass, and geothermal. These are clean, affordable, and reliable. Recently there has been a 70 – 80% reduction in the cost of solar. Currently energy demand is rising, making renewable energy most desirable. Wind and solar are readily available, but biomass must be produced. Biomass is an important source of renewable energy produced from trash, sugar, ethanol, and crop waste. It is renewable carbon, unlike fossil fuel.

The biggest challenge facing renewable energy is storage. The Apollo Energy Program is named after the Apollo Space program, which was responsible for putting a man on the moon. If it was possible for a man to land on, and return from, the moon, it should be possible to store renewable energy.

Successes in sustainable energy abound. Iceland obtains 100% of their electricity from renewable sources. KLM is the world's oldest airline, and uses 100% sustainable aviation fuel. KLM's biofuel comes from feedstock, and goes to airplanes. The Tessla electric car goes 400 kilometers on one charge of electricity. Tessla is better capitalized than General Motors.

Wallenberg's quality of compassion is applicable to the Climate Change and Sustainable Energy issues, and so are his qualities of courage and determination. It requires courage and determination to make, and implement, the decision to make a light carbon footprint. Please try it!

For more information:

UN Annual Department of Public Information NGO Climate Change Conference

United Nations Decade of Sustainable Energy Conference

People For the Ethical Treatment of Animals (PETA)

Chapter Forty-Eight: Choose Life

Many people have asked how I am related to Raoul Wallenberg. This was never important to me. Since there was so much interest, I decided to hire a detective in Stockholm. First he traced my Swedish grandfather, Eric Johan Wallenberg, forward and I found relatives I didn't know about in Stockholm. Later I visited them, and really enjoyed meeting them.

Next, the detective traced my Swedish grandfather backwards to a small village in northern Sweden where Raoul Wallenberg's ancestors came from. At that point he had to stop because the written records were not good. There probably is a family connection between my Swedish Grandfather and Raoul Wallenberg's family.

My situation is entirely different. I was adopted. My Daughter, who is a lawyer, was able to find my birth mother and her family. As it turns out, she was a teenage virgin when she was raped. I was conceived at approximately the same time Raoul Wallenberg was alleged to, and probably did, pass away in a Russian prison.

It is impossible to know now what Theresa's decision would have been if abortion had been legal then. Maybe, we would never know what happened to Raoul Wallenberg if Theresa chose to abort me, the product of conception resulting from her rape. She chose life. Raoul Wallenberg chose life for the 100,000 people he saved.

Now it is up to you to go forward attempting to emulate Raoul Wallenberg's compassion, courage, and determination. Above all, follow the advice of the Torah in Deuteronomy Chapter 30, verse 19: " I call heaven and earth to witness against you this day: I have put before you life and death, blessing and curse. *Choose life!*"

References For Part One:

"Righteous Gentile" by John Bierman

"With Raoul Wallenberg in Budapest" by Per Anger

"The Book That Disappeared" by Lars Berg

"Wallenberg The Man In The Iron Web" by Eleanor Lester

"Wallenberg" by Kati Marton

"Wallenberg: Lost Hero" by Danny Smith

As well as my conversations with Authors and Survivors, and my knowledge of Sweden through visits and relatives.

Appendix

<u>Correspondence</u>

Senator Claiborne Pell 12/5/89

Senator Daniel Patrick Moynihan 12/11/89

Congressman Robert J. Mrazek 12/19/89

Soviet Second Secretary Vladimir Parshikov 12/22/89

Soviet Official Boris A. Tsepov 5/15/90

Soviet Official Boris A. Tsepov 6/14/90

Senator Clairborne Pell 11/27/91

Senator Alfonse D'Amato 1/10/92

Elie Wiesel 10/19/88, 1/26/89, 9/25/89

Legislation

House Concurrent Resolution 165 (Mrazek)

Senate Concurrent Resolution 60 (Moynihan)

House Resolution 58 Congress (Lent)

Senate Resolution (D'Amato)

House Resolution 388 (McGrath)

101st CONGRESS
1st Session

H. CON. RES. 165

Expressing the sense of the Congress that the Soviet Union should release the prison records of Raoul Wallenberg and account for his whereabouts.

IN THE HOUSE OF REPRESENTATIVES

July 12, 1989

Mr. Mrazek (for himself, Mr. Towns, Mr. Clarke, Mr. Hochbrueckner, Ms. Pelosi, Mr. Ritter, Mr. Manton, Mr. Wolf, Mr. Gray, Mr. Rhodes, Mr. Sikorski, Mr. Solarz, Mr. Moakley, Mr. Durbin, Mr. Horton, Mr. Porter, Mr. Burton of Indiana, Mr. Gordon, Mr. Annunzio, Mrs. Unsoeld, Mr. Saxton, Mr. Dellums, Mrs. Collins, Mr. Rohrabacher, Mr. Olin, Mr. Lipinski, Mr. Fauntroy, Mr. Frank, Mr. Markey, Mr. Jacobs, Mr. DeFazio, Mr. Bryant, Mr. Ackerman, Mr. Scheuer, Mr. McNulty, Mr. Levine of California, Mrs. Morella, Mr. Matsui, Mr. Solomon, Mr. Lagomarsino, Mr. AuCoin, Mr. Torricelli, Mr. Morrison of Connecticut, Mr. Wheat, Mr. Evans, Mr. Campbell of Colorado, Mr. Gilman, Mr. Bilbray, Mr. Owens of Utah, Mr. Brown of Colorado, Mr. Lantos, Mr. Downey, Mr. McGrath, Mr. Wyden, Mr. Owens of New York, Mr. Bustamante, Mr. Leland, Mr. Inhofe, Mr. Kennedy, Mr. Atkins, Mr. Weber, Mr. McEwen, Mr. Kildee, Mr. Levin of Michigan, Mr. Bonior, Mr. Waxman, Mr. Kolter, Mr. Cox, Mr. Gejdenson, Mr. Edwards of Oklahoma, Mr. Fish, Mr. Weiss, and Mr. Lowery of California) submitted the following concurrent resolution; which was referred to the Committee on Foreign Affairs

---

CONCURRENT RESOLUTION

Expressing the sense of the Congress that the Soviet Union should release the prison records of Raoul Wallenberg and account for his whereabouts.

Whereas Raoul Wallenberg, a Swedish citizen and diplomat, was responsible for saving thousands of innocent people from being killed by the Nazis during World War II;

Whereas at the request of the United States War Refugee Board and the World Jewish Congress, Raoul Wallenberg went to Budapest in 1944 to organize rescue operations and save Hungarian Jews from being massacred in Nazi death camps;

Whereas Raoul Wallenberg used "protective passports" passes to save Hungarian Jews targeted for extermination in death camps in Eastern Europe from being executed;

Whereas Raoul Wallenberg courageously issued Swedish passports to more than 15,000 Jews and indirectly helped approximately 100,000 Hungarian Jews to escape Nazi plans for their extermination;

Whereas on January 17, 1945, Raoul Wallenberg was escorted by two Soviets to the Russian front, ostensibly to discuss arrangements for emergency supplies to be sent to the Jewish ghettos in Hungary, where he was taken into protective custody;

Whereas Raoul Wallenberg was arrested on charges of spying and taken by Soviet troops to the Lubianka Prison in Moscow and held there;

Whereas Raoul Wallenberg was taken into Soviet "protective custody" in violation of international standards of diplomatic immunity;

Whereas the Soviets claim that Raoul Wallenberg died in a Soviet prison in 1947 at the age of 35 of a heart attack, but neither his remains nor any other evidence of his death have ever been produced by the Soviets to verify his death;

●HCON 105 III

3

Whereas there have been a number of sightings and accounts of
Raoul Wallenberg that indicate that he may still be alive
and in Soviet custody;

Whereas the Soviet Union refuses to investigate the reports that
Raoul Wallenberg is still alive;

Whereas the contribution of Raoul Wallenberg to the fight for
human rights and against the Nazi-orchestrated holocaust
must be acknowledged; and

Whereas the truth about the whereabouts of Raoul Wallenberg
must be made public: Now, therefore, be it

1   *Resolved by the House of Representatives (the Senate*
2   *concurring),* That the Congress requests—

3   (1) that the Soviet Union release the prison
4   records of Raoul Wallenberg and account for his
5   whereabouts; and

6   (2) that the President pursue, through diplomatic
7   actions with the Soviet Union, such release and
8   accounting.

○

1   *Resolved by the Senate (the House of Representatives*
2   *concurring),* That the Senate requests—

3   (1) that the Soviet Union release the prison
4   records of Raoul Wallenberg and account for his
5   whereabouts; and

6   (2) that the President pursue, through diplomatic
7   actions with the Soviet Union, such release and ac-
8   counting.

○

SCON 60 IS

United States Senate

COMMITTEE ON FOREIGN RELATIONS

WASHINGTON, DC 20510-6225

December 5, 1989

Ms. Sharon L. Wallenberg
President
The Raoul Wallenberg Committee of
  Long Island
P.O. Box 45
46 Brown Street
Sea Cliff, New York 11579

Dear Ms. Wallenberg:

Thank you for your letter concerning S. Con. Res. 60.

As you know, I continue to have a deep personal inter[
the case of Raoul Wallenberg. His acts of courage were ha
of true heroism, and it is most distressing that, to this
remain uncertain of his fate.

As a cosponsor of S. Con. Res. 60, I appreciate your
the proposed changes to my attention. My staff has been i
with Senator Moynihan's office to be sure that the matter
handled appropriately when the bill is considered by the S
Foreign Relations Committee next year.

With every good wish.

Ever sincerely,

Claiborne Pell

389

DANIEL P. MOYNIHAN
NEW YORK

United States Senate
WASHINGTON, DC 20510

December 11, 1989

Dear Mrs. Wallenberg:

Many thanks for writing to offer additions to S. Con. Res. 60. In view of the recent Soviet effort to resolve the case of Raoul Wallenberg, your suggestions are quite fitting.

According to Senate procedure, a bill that has been referred to committee -- such as S. Con. Res. 60 -- can be amended both in committee and on the Senate floor. Although we have gathered a large number of co-sponsors for the resolution in its present form, I believe that your suggestions have merit and will seek support for modifications. I look forward to passing the resolution early in the new year.

Again, I do thank you for keeping in touch. Please continue to do so.

Sincerely,

Daniel Patrick Moynihan

Sharon L. Wallenberg
46 Brown Street
Sea Cliff, NY 11579

CONGRESS OF THE UNITED STATES
HOUSE OF REPRESENTATIVES
WASHINGTON, D.C. 20515

ROBERT J. MRAZEK
3RD DISTRICT, NEW YORK

COMMITTEE ON
APPROPRIATIONS
WHIP AT LARGE

December 19, 1989

Ms. Sharon L. Wallenberg
President
The Raoul Wallenberg Committee
of Long Island
P.O. Box 45
Sea Cliff, New York 11579

Dear Sharon:

Thank you for your recent letters concerning an amendment to the
Wallenberg amendment, H. Con. Res. 165.

I certainly agree that advances by the Soviets with regard to this case
call for some kind of re-evaluation of the resolution in its present
form. I will be spending time with my family during the holidays, but
on my return to Washington, I will speak to the appropriate subcommittee chairmen on the Foreign Affairs Committee and then determine how we
should proceed.

Again, thank you for your helpful suggestions.

Sincerely,

Bob Mrazek

Robert J. Mrazek
Member of Congress

RJM:cab

United States Senate
WASHINGTON, DC 20510

January 10, 1992

H.E. Anders Ingemar Thunborg
Ambassador Extraordinary and Plenipotentiary
Embassy of Sweden
Suites 715 and 1200
600 New Hampshire Ave.
Washington, DC 20037

Dear Ambassador Thunborg:

I am writing to seek a clarification of the official Swedish government position on the fate of Raoul Wallenberg.

It has been brought to my attention that there appears to be a certain inconsistency in statements by Swedish officials concerning Mr. Wallenberg. Some government representatives seem to have flatly accused the Soviets of lying about his death, while others give every indication of having accepted the explanation that Wallenberg died in prison. What is the official Swedish government position on Raoul Wallenberg?

I would appreciate your help in resolving the confusion over this issue that has long been of deep interest to both our nations.

Sincerely,

Alfonse M. D'Amato
United States Senator

AMD:gjr

United States Senate
WASHINGTON, DC 20510-3202

January 29, 1992

Ms. Sharon Wallenberg
President, The Raoul Wallenberg Committee
  of Long Island, Inc.
46 Brown Street, Post Office Box 45
Sea Cliff, NY 11579

Dear Ms. Wallenberg:

Please find enclosed, a copy of the
letter I received from the Swedish Embassy
answering my inquiry as to the official
Swedish government position on Mr.
Wallenberg.

Sincerely,

Alfonse M. D'Amato
United States Senator

AMD:gjr

393

Washington, January 24, 1992

The Honorable Alfonse M. D'Amato
United States Senate
Washington, D.C. 20510

Sir:

With reference to your letter of January 10, 1992,
I have the pleasure to enclose a brochure about
Raoul Wallenberg.

The official Swedish position is: "As long as we
have not been presented with irrefutable evidence
on the contrary, we consider Raoul Wallenberg to be
alive".

Sincerely,

Lena Kjellström
Second Secretary

Address	Telephone	Telegram	Telex
Suite 1200	(202) 944-5600	Svensk	RCA 248347, SVSK UR
600 New Hampshire Avenue, N. W.			WU 89-2724 SVENSK WSH
WASHINGTON, D. C. 20037			
USA			

102 CONGRESS

2nd SESSION

S. RES. _____

(Note.—Fill in all blank lines except those provided for the date, number, and reference of resolution.)

IN THE SENATE OF THE UNITED STATES

Mr. D'Amato, Lieberman, Moynihan, Spector, Cohen

submitted the following resolution; which was _____

RESOLUTION

Expressing the sense of the Senate that the United States should seek a final and conclusive account of the whereabouts and definitive fate of Raoul Wallenberg.

Whereas Raoul Wallenberg, a Swedish citizen and diplomat, was responsible for saving the lives of 15,000 Hungarian Jews through the issuance of Swedish passports, and helping a further 100,000 Hungarian Jews escape Nazi authorities during World War II;

Whereas on January 17, 1945, Raoul Wallenberg was taken into "protective custody" by Soviet troops, in violation of all international standards of diplomatic immunity;

Whereas Raoul Wallenberg was later arrested by Soviet troops on charges of spying, and finally taken to Lubyanka Prison in Moscow, where he was reported to have died on July 17, 1947 of a heart attack;

Whereas conflicting reports and information has surfaced over the last forty-four years claiming that Raoul Wallenberg was executed by Soviet authorities or in fact is still alive in the former Soviet Union;

Whereas the Soviet Union has now ceased to exist and has been succeeded by the Commonwealth of Independent States which has pursued democratic reform while seeking to address Soviet atrocities of the past;

Whereas the time has come to finally put an end to all speculation and confusion as to the fate of Raoul Wallenberg: Now, therefore, be it

Resolved, That the Senate--

(1) gratefully acknowledges the cooperation of the Soviet and now Russian authorities in providing records and personal effects of Raoul Wallenberg to his family;

(2) requests that the President of the United States pursue, through diplomatic discussions with the government of the Russian Federation, an investigation into the whereabouts and definitive fate of Raoul Wallenberg;

(3) requests that the results of this investigation be made public.

102nd Congress
1st Session

H.Con.Res. 58

IN THE HOUSE OF REPRESENTATIVES

Mr. Lent introduced the following concurrent resolution; which
was referred to the Committee on _____

CONCURRENT RESOLUTION

Expressing the sense of the Congress that the Soviet Union
should release the prison records of Raoul Wallenberg and account
for his whereabouts.

WHEREAS Raoul Wallenberg, a Swedish citizen and diplomat,
was responsible for saving thousands of innocent people from
being killed by the Nazis during World War II;

WHEREAS at the request of the United States War Refugee
Board and the World Jewish Congress, Raoul Wallenberg went to
Budapest in 1944 to organize rescue operations and save Hungarian
Jews from being massacred by the Nazis;

WHEREAS Raoul Wallenberg used "protective passports" as
passes to save Hungarian Jews targeted for extermination in death
camps in Eastern Europe;

102nd Congress
1st Session

H.Con.Res. 58

IN THE HOUSE OF REPRESENTATIVES

Mr. Lent introduced the following concurrent resolution; which
was referred to the Committee on _____

CONCURRENT RESOLUTION

Expressing the sense of the Congress that the Soviet Union
should release the prison records of Raoul Wallenberg and account
for his whereabouts.

WHEREAS Raoul Wallenberg, a Swedish citizen and diplomat,
was responsible for saving thousands of innocent people from
being killed by the Nazis during World War II;

WHEREAS at the request of the United States War Refugee
Board and the World Jewish Congress, Raoul Wallenberg went to
Budapest in 1944 to organize rescue operations and save Hungarian
Jews from being massacred by the Nazis;

WHEREAS Raoul Wallenberg used "protective passports" as
passes to save Hungarian Jews targeted for extermination in death
camps in Eastern Europe;

102D CONGRESS
2D SESSION

H. RES. 388

Expressing the sense of the House of Representatives that the United States should seek a final and conclusive account of the whereabouts and definitive fate of Raoul Wallenberg.

IN THE HOUSE OF REPRESENTATIVES

MARCH 4, 1992

Mr. McGRATH for himself, submitted the following resolution; which was referred to the Committee on Foreign Affairs

---

RESOLUTION

Expressing the sense of the House of Representatives that the United States should seek a final and conclusive account of the whereabouts and definitive fate of Raoul Wallenberg.

Whereas Raoul Wallenberg, a Swedish citizen and diplomat, was responsible for saving the lives of fifteen thousand Hungarian Jews through the issuance of Swedish passports, and helping a further one hundred thousand Hungarian Jews escape Nazi authorities during World War II;

Whereas, on January 17, 1945, Raoul Wallenberg was taken into "protective custody" by Soviet troops, in violation of all international standards of diplomatic immunity;

Whereas Raoul Wallenberg was later arrested by Soviet troops on charges of spying, and finally taken to Lubyanka Prison in Moscow, where he was reported to have died on July 17, 1947, of a heart attack;

Whereas conflicting reports and information has surfaced over the last forty-four years claiming that Raoul Wallenberg was executed by Soviet authorities or in fact is still alive in the former Soviet Union;

Whereas the Soviet Union has now ceased to exist and has been succeeded by the Commonwealth of Independent States which has pursued democratic reform while seeking to address Soviet atrocities of the past; and

Whereas the time has come to finally put an end to all speculation and confusion as to the fate of Raoul Wallenberg: Now, therefore, be it

1 *Resolved,* That the House of Representatives—

2 (1) gratefully acknowledges the cooperation of
3 the Soviet and now Russian authorities in providing
4 records and personal effects of Raoul Wallenberg to
5 his family;

6 (2) requests that the President of the United
7 States pursue, through diplomatic discussions with
8 the Government of the Russian Federation, an inves-
9 tigation into the whereabouts and definitive fate of
10 Raoul Wallenberg; and

11 (3) requests that the results of this investiga-
12 tion be made public.

○

103rd Congress
1st Session

H.J.Res._____

IN THE UNITED STATES HOUSE OF REPRESENTATIVES

Mr. King, submitted the following resolution; which was

Expressing the sense of the House that the United States should
seek a final and conclusive account of the whereabouts and
definitive fate of Raoul Wallenberg.

Whereas Raoul Wallenberg, a Swedish citizen and diplomat, was
    responsible for saving the lives of 15,000 Hungarian Jews
    through the issuance of Swedish passports, and helping a
    further 100,000 Hungarian Jews escape Nazi authorities during
    World War II;

Whereas on January 17, 1945, Raoul Wallenberg was taken into
    "protective custody" by Soviet troops, in violation of all
    international standards of diplomatic immunity;

Whereas Raoul Wallenberg was later arrested by Soviet troops on
    charges of spying, and finally taken to Lubyanka Prison in
    Moscow, where he was reported to have died on July 17, 1947
    of a heart attack;

Whereas conflicting reports and information has surfaced over the
    last forty-four years claiming that Raoul Wallenberg was
    executed by Soviet authorities or in fact is still alive in
    the former Soviet Union;

Whereas the Soviet Union has now ceased to exist and has been
    succeeded by the Commonwealth of Independent States which has
    pursued democratic reform while seeking to address Soviet
    atrocities of the past;

Whereas the time has come to finally put an end to all
    speculation and confusion as to the fate of Raoul Wallenberg:
    Now, therefore, be it

    Resolved, That the House--

    (1) gratefully acknowledges the cooperation of the Soviet
    and now Russian authorities in providing records and personal
    effects of Raoul Wallenberg to his family;

400

(2) requests that the President of the United States pursue,
through diplomatic discussions with the government of the
Russian Federation, an investigation into the whereabouts and
definitive fate of Raoul Wallenberg;

(3) requests that the results of this investigation be made
public.

ПОСТОЯННОЕ ПРЕДСТАВИТЕЛЬСТВО
СОЮЗА СОВЕТСКИХ СОЦИАЛИСТИЧЕСКИХ
РЕСПУБЛИК
ПРИ
ОРГАНИЗАЦИИ ОБЪЕДИНЕННЫХ НАЦИЙ

PERMANENT MISSION
OF THE UNION OF SOVIET SOCIALIST
REPUBLICS
TO THE UNITED NATIONS
136 East 67th Street
New York, N. Y. 10021

Mrs. Sharon L.WALLENBERG
Post Office Box 45-46 Brown Street
Sea Cliff, New York 11579

New York, December 22 , 1989

Dear Sharon,

Please find enclosed a copy of an article
"Is the Case of Raoul Wallenberg Closed?", published
in the December issue of a Soviet magazine "Mezhdunarodnaya
Zhizn" ("International Life").

I believe you'll find it interesting.

Please accept my best wishes for health and happiness
in the New Year.

Sincerely yours,

Vladimir Parshikov

VLADIMIR A. PARSHIKOV
SECOND SECRETARY
PERMANENT MISSION OF THE U.S.S.R.
TO THE UNITED NATIONS

(212) 861-4900

136 EAST 67TH STREET
NEW YORK, NY 10021

402

ПОСТОЯННОЕ ПРЕДСТАВИТЕЛЬСТВО
СОЮЗА СОВЕТСКИХ СОЦИАЛИСТИЧЕСКИХ
РЕСПУБЛИК
ПРИ
ОРГАНИЗАЦИИ ОБЪЕДИНЕННЫХ НАЦИЙ

PERMANENT MISSION
OF THE UNION OF SOVIET SOCIALIST
REPUBLICS
TO THE UNITED NATIONS
136 East 67th Street
New York, N. Y. 10021

Sharon L.WALLENBERG
President,
The Raoul Wallenberg Committee
of Long Island
P.O.Box 45, 46 Brown Street
Sea Cliff, New York 11579

May 15, 1990

Dear Sharon:

Thank you very much for the photo and letter dated May 7, 1990.

I was really very pleased to join you, your colleagues and friends that night, to pay tribute to heroic deeds of Raoul Wallenberg. The photo and the letter will remind me the party at the Swan Club.

Hope to see you in August.

Sincerely,

Boris A.TSEPOV

ПОСТОЯННОЕ ПРЕДСТАВИТЕЛЬСТВО
СОЮЗА СОВЕТСКИХ СОЦИАЛИСТИЧЕСКИХ
РЕСПУБЛИК
ПРИ
ОРГАНИЗАЦИИ ОБЪЕДИНЕННЫХ НАЦИЙ

PERMANENT MISSION
OF THE UNION OF SOVIET SOCIALIST
REPUBLICS
TO THE UNITED NATIONS
136 East 67th Street
New York, N. Y. 10021

New York, June 14, 1990

Dear Sharon:

Thank you for your letter of June 2, 1990. I also believe that all doubts and uncertainties connected with the fate of Raoul Wallenberg should be dissolved. You may be sure that the USSR Mission to the U.N. stays ready to provide the R.W.C. of L.I. with an assisiance necessary to reach its humane goals.

Concerning your very kind suggestion to join the list of dignitaries on the committee's letterhead. Believe me it would be really a great honour for us to be placed on your committee letterhead together with the others Honorary Chairmen of R.W.C. of L.I. But as the Soviet diplomats posted abroad we should follow the rules of our diplomatic service which unfortunately do not enable us to accept a suggestion of that kind. I hope you understand the delicate character of our official status and accept our regrets.

To certain extent I write this letter on behalf of Mr. Valentin Lozinski and Mr. Dmitri Bykov. Both of them are vocationing now back home in Moscow and are to be here again in the middle of July.

I remain faithfully yours.

Boris A. TSEPOV

United States Senate

COMMITTEE ON FOREIGN RELATIONS

WASHINGTON, DC 20510-6225

November 27, 1991

Ms. Sharon Wallenberg
46 Brown Street
Sea Cliff, New York   11579

Dear Ms. Wallenberg:

Thank you for your letter and the enclosed material about Raoul Wallenberg.

I do not have any information that would explain the apparent contradiction between the actions and the statements of the Government of Sweden or of Raoul Wallenberg's relatives. It may be that privately both have accepted the Soviets claim that Wallenberg is dead but publicly they do not want to admit that this may be the case.

With every good wish.

Ever sincerely,

Claiborne Pell
Chairman

405

Boston University

University Professors
745 Commonwealth Avenue
Boston, Massachusetts 02215
617/353-4566
FAX 617-353-5084
Elie Wiesel, *Andrew W. Mellon Professor in the Humanities*

October 19, 1988

Ms. Sharon Wallenberg
P. O. Box 45
Sea Cliff, NY 11579

Dear Ms. Wallenberg:

Thanks for your letter. I appreciate being informed regarding activities on behalf of Raoul Wallenberg.

We need to have access to the official Raoul Wallenberg file; it contains elements of information that his friends deserve to know.

With best wishes, I am,

Sincerely yours,

Elie Wiesel

EW/mlh

Boston University

University Professors
745 Commonwealth Avenue
Boston, Massachusetts 02215
617/353-4566

Elie Wiesel, *Andrew W. Mellon Professor in the Humanities*

1·26·89

Dear Sharon Walbensey —

Thank you for your good
wans. I agree: first we must
obtain the secret f.b. What to
do with it is another question —
that can wait.

Lecture? Yes — but my schedule
is already too heavy for this
academic year —

All the best to you —

Elie Wiesel

407

Boston University

University Professors
745 Commonwealth Avenue
Boston, Massachusetts 02215
617/353-4566

Elie Wiesel, *Andrew W. Mellon Professor in the Humanities*

9. 25. 89

Dear Sharon —

When you come
back — will you tell
me of the conversations
you have had in
Moscow?

A happy new year
to you —

Elie Wiesel

408

Printed in Great Britain
by Amazon